THE TRUE
MAGICIAN HARRY WISE

A WIZARD'S
TUX AND TALES

CHARLIE CARLSON

For ~~Mickey Pear~~, my Canadian Buddy (I hope!!)

LUTHERS
NEW SMYRNA BEACH
F L O R I D A

11/1/04

PRINTED IN THE UNITED STATES OF AMERICA

COVER PHOTOS COURTESY OF
Tommy Vincent
Seminole Herald
Sanford, Florida

ISBN: 1-877633-70-4

Published by
LUTHERS
1009 North Dixie Freeway
New Smyrna Beach, FL 32168-6221
www.lutherspublishing.com

Contents

❖❖❖❖❖❖❖❖❖❖❖❖

Chapter 1
How it all started. Page 1

Chapter 2
Turning professional, Mr. Old Stag, and the Ritz. Page 5

Chapter 3
The first big national tour with Johnny Cates. Page 19

Chapter 4
Mr. Magic on television. Page 29

Chapter 5
Dr. Jekyl's Weird Show. Page 35

Chapter 6
On the road with the show. Page 43

Chapter 7
The big magic show. Page 53

Chapter 8
Mind Reading. Page 63

Chapter 9
The Magical Circus Ringmaster. Page 69

Chapter 10
The mystic world of dreams and unicorns. Page 75

Chapter 11
A legend in the Wizard's words. Page 81

Selected Works by H. W. Wise Pages 86, 87 and 88

For Helen Margaret Voglar Wise and Alton W. "Doc" Wise, my parents, who said we'll help you in any way we can to become a magician and showman...and they did. Thanks for a wonderful life. I wasn't off to see the Wizard....I was off to be the Wizard!

H. W. W.

Chapter 1

"You can't reveal the secrets...unless you want to feel the wrath of the wizard's wand...and who wants to be turned into a toad?"
The Author

I can still remember as if it happened yesterday, yet so many years have gone by since that extraordinary day at Westside Primary School. I'm talking about the most amazing thing that I had ever seen in my life, well, at least up to the fourth grade. But before I get into this story, you need to know something about where this happened.

About thirty miles north of America's theme park capital of Orlando, Florida, sits a waterfront town called Sanford. It was founded in 1877 by Henry Sanford who dubbed it "The Gate City of South Florida." By the turn of the century, this was a bustling hub for railroads and steamboats bringing the first vacationers to Central Florida. Actually, it is where all of Central Florida's history began, including the first theater and even the first amusement park, called "Woodland Park." Of course, this was long before anybody ever thought about such places as Sea World, Disney World, and all those other worlds.

Sanford was a typical small Southern town at the head of navigation on the St. Johns river. Okay, maybe not quite so typical. The truth is, there was such a mixture of nationalities here that the place should have been the seat for the United Nations. Most of these folks were immigrants but the rest were an assortment of characters that included entrepreneurs, ex-spies from both sides of the Civil War, carpetbaggers, scallywags, a couple of mediums, cattlemen, river men, moonshiners, railroaders, and a few eccentric folks. Actually, we had more than our share of eccentric folks and still do. Eccentric? Well...that's just a nice way of saying weird and mysterious. Still, this was a place where everybody knew their neighbors...which made it hard for a kid to get into trouble. You know what I'm talking about, old houses with porches, moss-drenched live oaks lining brick streets, and a clothes line in every backyard...that sort of thing. As a matter of fact, Sanford looks just like that little Pennsylvania town in the movie "My Girl." It should, because Sanford is where the movie was filmed as well as being the setting for several other movies and TV commercials. In 1960, NBC filmed a television series here called "The Big Tent" and half the folks in town showed up to be in it but nobody can remember ever seeing it on television. Most likely, you've seen our town on the silver-screen without even knowing it. Of course, if you stayed in the theater long enough to read the credits, then you might have seen the name where it says something like, "filmed on location in Sanford, Florida."

However, the glamour of Hollywood is not really Sanford's claim to fame. Actually, we were world famous for celery. That's right, "celery!" Prior to 1940, just about every stalk of celery that was ever consumed in the United States and Canada came from Sanford. That's about 6000 boxcar loads each year and I'm still mystified at how people could eat so much celery. Today, the celery fields have long been replaced by shopping centers, apartment complexes, and asphalt parking lots. Sanford's main street, lined with its antique shops and quaint eateries, is now listed on the National Historic Register. I know a few of our residents who should be on that register too. Even the old Ritz theater building, where I once saw cowboy matinees every Saturday, has been restored, and across the street, still standing proudly, is the old Imperial Opera House building. Both are reminders of when the town was a center of entertainment during the days of vaudeville, concerts, minstrels, and other live stage shows. For me, the most shocking live performances came later in the form of midnight ghost shows during the fifties and sixties at the Ritz. All the kids in town flocked to these live stage shows that were usually held on Halloween night. For those who could endure these scary exhibitions, the Ritz would issue free passes to a future movie. I got one of those free passes when I went to see

Dr. Jekyl's Weird Show. That was the time when the mad Doctor plucked me and some other boys out of the audience to participate on stage with him. We were what magicians call a "stooge." In my case, I was familiar with the term as it had often been used by one of my teachers. It was at this particular show that I discovered a link between the eerie Doctor Jekyl and a mesmerizing experience a few years earlier at Westside Primary School...which is where this story really begins.

I was in the fourth grade at Westside when we were marched to our little auditorium for a special assembly. I figured it was going to be another one of those sing-a-long sessions with one of the teachers banging out tunes on the old upright piano. As soon as we filed in to take our seats I sensed that this was going to be something really different. Even that old piano had been rolled out of the way to the corner of the stage. On the tiny stage were some mysterious apparatuses unlike anything I had ever seen before. I remember seeing a weird looking table with a pretty covering and some other strange gadgets that I could not readily identify.

After we were seated, Mrs. Watt, the second grade teacher, walked down in front and, in her grandmotherly manner, warned us to keep our seats, sit up straight, and to behave ourselves, and we would be in for a real surprise. With that said, she proceeded to introduce a neatly dressed gentleman who had walked out on stage. It was the Wizard himself! The very first magician I had ever seen. His eyes immediately scanned the audience capturing the mind of every pupil. We all sat still, as if under the spell of this wizard, as he began making things materialize out of nowhere...then disappear into thin air. He made colorful silks change colors and turned a ball into two balls, then into three balls. I had never seen anything like it. I always knew our teachers were smart, but they couldn't do stuff like this; it was no wonder they wanted us to see this marvelous, science-defying demonstration. He even cut a rope into pieces then with a wave of his wand the pieces became a single rope again! All this stuff was being done before our very eyes and it sure beat studying arithmetic! We were witnessing great feats of conjuring, convinced that these miracles were somehow caused by that magical wand he was waving around. It was a short performance, but long in our memories. I tried my best to remember everything so I could tell my parents. I said to myself, "They're never gonna believe this stuff."

I figured that if I had one of those wands, I could do magic like that wizard I saw at school. I went home and tried to make a wand from a hickory stick, but it didn't work; at least, not like that one the Wizard used on the stage at Westside Primary School. That astonishing exhibition had taught all of us a good lesson, that only wizards have real wands.

I recently flipped through my cheap dictionary and found the word "wizard" defined as "A person with magical skills and powers." It also said that a wizard is a magician. I then looked-up "magician" and found it defined as "One who performs tricks and illusions that seem impossible." Therefore, I conclude that a thin veil separates a wizard from a magician. But who among us can really distinguish a wizard from a magician? After all, the majority of folks are not privileged to the secrets of how things are done. A magician, or wizard, exists in two worlds, the one we see on stage...and the mysterious one behind the curtain, or backstage, where average folks never get to go.

The magician I had witnessed was the *Great Harry Wise* who went on to carry his wizardry to American audiences coast-to-coast and into Canada. Years later our paths would cross several times. The first time was at the Ritz, in that crazy Doctor Jekyl spook show, when I discovered the mad doctor was the same fellow who had held us spellbound at Westside Primary. Decades later, when I was booking carnival midways for army bases, producing bluegrass music festivals, and dabbling in my own version of show business, I ran into the Great Wizard again. He had just finished a tour as the magical ringmaster for a circus. He was a little worn from years on the showbiz trail, but along the way, he had packed more experiences under his cape than the average human will have in ten lifetimes. And yes, his wand still worked. We spent some time in a Sanford city park exchanging show business tales...in carnival lingo it's called "cuttin' jackpots." We had things in common, for starters, we both loved circuses and carnivals, and could "talk-the-talk." When you have things in common with a wizard you can learn secrets that most people will never know. The problem is, you can't reveal the secrets...unless you want to feel the wrath of the wizard's wand...and who wants to be turned into a toad? Certainly not me. Although I'm sure Harry Wise would consider it a spectacular feat of conjuration worthy of an audience.

Chapter 2

"I've got to be that man on that stage...in that tux doing that magic...talking to that audience and making them laugh."
Harry Wise, 15 years old

Harry Wise, the only son of *Alton* and *Helen Wise*, was born in 1934 on east 6th Street in Sanford, Florida. Wise the Wizard gets his name from his grandfather, *Harry William Wise*, who ventured down from Lewiston, Maine, in 1905 and opened Sanford's first restaurant in 1907.

There's an uncanny parallel between the name of Harry Wise and the famous escape artist, *Harry Houdini*. In 1891, Houdini changed his name from *Ehrich Weiss*, a surname translated as "Wise." Like Harry Houdini, Harry Wise performed under names other than his original moniker and this is where the first secret is revealed in this book. What most people do not know, is that the following stage personalities, Mr. Magic, Doctor Jekyl, the Amazing Hans Voglar, Dark Veil, Darkvale, Old Mr. Stag and, of course, Wise the Wizard, were really the same man...Harry Wise.

Harry's father, Alton, had spent some time as a roustabout with a traveling carnival and later operated a shooting gallery before settling down to a career as a house painter.

In 1943, Alton Wise moved his family to a wood frame house on west 6th Street. It was here that Harry Wise the entertainer grew up. Today this dwelling is the Wizard's domain, filled with over fifty-years of magic and fantasy.

It is a place where every day is Halloween, where mystery literally permeates the air; where fantasy and reality are separated only by a thin veil. It is a genuine conjurer's museum filled with stage props, talking skulls, top hats, silks, secrets, and show posters from hundreds of theaters. It is a time-machine of sorts, guarded by unseen unicorns, where the future and the past are rolled into the present...or maybe the present is really the past...or whatever you want it to be.

I have been one of a privileged few invited into the Wizard's domain in which I can only tell you that I saw things that you can only imagine. I realized that behind the curtain of this strange world was a real story that needed to be told.

I made arrangements for a clandestine rendezvous with the Wizard at the local H & M Restaurant. Well, it wasn't quite so clandestine since everybody in the place knew Harry Wise...although few knew him beyond the city limits, and none knew what I was about to find out through a series of interviews over the next couple of months.

I walked into the restaurant and immediately saw my subject wave for me to join him at his table in the back corner. He was in everyday street clothes, no top hat or cape, but his long, white hair and beard would've made anyone assume that he was either Saint Nick or a wizard. I took a seat and ordered a cup of coffee as he proceeded to shuffle through a pile of old pictures and newspaper clippings that were testimony to his fifty years of mystifying people all over the country. After looking through this small archive of theatrical history I was inspired to ask, "Okay, so tell me, why'd you to want to be a magician?"

He took a sip of his coffee and sat it down beside an old theater poster, and gently stroking his white beard, he drifted back through space and time, to his starting point.

"You have to understand," he began to explain. "This really goes back to when I was five or six. I always loved radio and the movies...any kind of show business...and Dad would always take us to any carnival that came to town. He was a legionnaire, and the American Legion always sponsored the Seminole County Fair in town and he was on the committee taking tickets at the front gate...or one of the shows or whatever. He would always take us out there to the Fair two or three nights. But, in 1944, when I was ten years old, Dad took us to the Wallace Brothers circus that was playing right down there on the lakefront. Now this was a wonderful show in the

Sanford, Florida, birthplace of a wizard. [Courtesy of The Sanford Museum]

forties, and I saw all those beautiful ladies, and...trapeze artists, animals, and the clowns, and acrobats, and I was really enchanted. But that afternoon on the way home after the circus, we had to go to the A&P store to do some grocery shopping. Now I didn't want to leave that circus...that canvas tent, and the smell of it and sights of it. At ten years old I knew that something must be wrong with the world because we were leaving the circus to go to a grocery store! The A&P was right across the street from the Ritz Theater...and I'm following my mother and dad up and down the aisles of that store wondering what is wrong with this. I wanted to be back there at the circus with all those beautiful girls, the glamour, the animals, and acrobats. Oh...I felt so depressed, it really upset me. Needless to say I couldn't hardly sleep that night thinking about that circus.

"The next day I got up early and rode my bicycle down to the lakefront, to the circus...but it was gone! There was just an empty lot with some holes where the tent stakes had been. I mean, you couldn't even tell it had been there...men, trucks, animals, the tents, everything was gone. It had vanished like magic. My heart sank. I went home, and Dad could tell something was wrong with me because I was moping around. He sat me down and explained that a circus was a one-day event and they go from town to town...and he explained the whole schematic to me. Well, I then knew more about it, but I knew then at ten that I wanted to do something in show business...but as yet had not discovered magic. When I discovered magic...there was no stopping me, trust me."

In 1948, Harry Wise saw his first magic show, *Wong Fu the Magician,* at the local junior high school. Wong Fu was always decked-out in Chinese attire, but other than that, there was nothing oriental about this showman. Wong Fu was really William Beech, a magician who worked school assemblies all over the Southeast.

In 1949, *Bill Neff and his Madhouse of Mystery* played the local Ritz Theater and young Harry Wise was in the audience. Neff was one of the top stage showmen in the country and the brother-in-law of actor Jimmie Stewart. His *Madhouse of Mystery* was what was called a live ghost show, featuring stage magic, scary illusions, and a total blackout of the theater.

Ghost shows, or horror shows, were popular live stage performances in theaters from the thirties into the sixties and usually preceded the showing of a scary movie. The producers of these stage shows were called "ghost masters." The old spook shows are now extinct, but are considered by some showbiz historians as the last remnants of vaudeville. What Harry Wise did not know as a kid in the audience, was that he would help close the final curtains of vaudeville as one of America's last performing ghost masters.

"I remember seeing those shows," recalled Wise. "But I wasn't to discover the world I was looking for until a year later, in April 1950...when I was fifteen. My parents took me to the Ritz Theater to see *Doctor Silkini and his Asylum of Horrors.* That was a midnight ghost show on stage with a blackout and monsters that roamed out on the stage. Doctor Silkini did a little magic, he opened with some flash magic and did a trick or two with kids up from the audience. And here I am, sitting there in the audience seeing this handsome man doing miracles on that stage with two beautiful women. Now I knew these were tricks, but at fifteen it didn't look like a trick. He had this long, shiny, silver tube, called a genie tube. You open it to show the audience it's empty...then snap it back close and it produces beautiful silk scarves. He tossed those rainbow-colored silks into mid-air as they came out of that tube and the girls would grab them. I knew I wanted to do that. He had on that beautiful tux and I knew I had to have that tux and that tube. Oh it was so flamboyant!

"Silkini was the show where I really caught the show bug because I got to go up on stage, as a stooge, and help out.

A show herald advertising Dr. Silkini's "Asylum of Horrors."

[Author's collection]

The Ritz theater in Sanford, Florida originally opened in August 1923 as the Milane, and was built on the site of an 1887 theater called the Star. The historic Ritz has been restored and is now used for plays.
[Sanford Museum]

"I was the 'hot seat boy'. Silkini says to me, 'Go back there to that lady and she will tell you what to do'. She told me what to do and says get back there behind the curtain. So, I'm back there waiting behind the curtain, and they bring the monster out on stage to do his bit...and then they do the blackout...turned the lights out in the theater. Then the lights came back on and Silkini looks around for me and pretends he can't find me. Then he pulls up that curtain and I'm in there flapping that curtain around looking like an idiot and the audience just died laughing. The audience just lost it. Of course, everybody knew me. But when those folks laughed at me being the boy behind the curtain trying to get away from the monster, well...something came over me at that moment. I felt like I was part of that show even though I was just a stooge. I made up my mind right then that I was going to make people laugh and was going to fool them...and be just like Silkini. Years later I would learn that Doctor Silkini was really Jack Baker out of Toledo, Ohio, and those two beautiful girls were his wife, Margie, and his sister-in-law.

"Walking home after the show that night, I told my parents 'I've got to be that man on that stage...in that tux doing that magic...talking to that audience and making them laugh, and I've got to have one or two beautiful girls to be with me'.

"The next week, we sat on the front porch and came up with a plan. I couldn't stand school, I thought I was far more intelligent than most of my teachers. So Dad told me that if I would drop out of high school and paint houses with him, he and Mother would endorse me fully in what I wanted to do in life...that of being a magician and showman. I could take the money I made from painting houses and invest it in my own show, but I had to be in at ten at night. That meant no bumming around with my bummy friends, and I did have a few which I won't name, but I had five or six of them. So, I dropped out of school and Dad took me to sign papers so the truant officer wouldn't be coming to the house looking for me.

"I started painting houses and sending my money to "Little Lulu" comic books, and "Archie" comic books. You've seen those ads that say...'send fifty-cents for our catalog, be the life of the party, learn magic' and all that. Well I'm in all the way, I'm sending thirty-five cents, a quarter, fifty-cents...I still have every catalog that I ordered from fifty years ago. I sent off for several tricks, the first one was color changing scarves.

"I used to stand in front of the mirror doing that color changing scarf thing...it was beautiful, and there's nothing to it! I was just fascinated with myself. Next, I ordered the egg bag...where you do the whole routine, the egg appears and disappears and all that. It's a good routine...I still have my egg bag and do it in some of my shows. Now my first audience was my family and our neighbors. Dad and Mother would have the neighbors over for dinner, or Canasta, it was the big game in those days, or to play Chinese checkers, and I would bore them with my latest tricks. During this time I was still painting houses, that was in fifty-one and fifty-two, and I'm getting magic stuff shipped in from magic shops all over, Pennsylvania and Chicago, the Magician's Company in Winwood, Pennsylvania, Douglas Magicland in Dallas, Texas...I was getting stuff left and right. At this time, I had about five or six hundred dollars invested in all this. I pretty much put all my pay into magic, of course, I kept enough to go to the movies.

"One day, Dad and I was sitting on the porch and he said, 'Harry maybe you ought to try to book a show or something.' I said, 'Well I don't know, I'll talk to somebody.' Now in 1953, I did work two birthday parties for seven dollars and fifty-cents. But I don't consider those the start of my professional career, that got started on Friday, October 30th, 1953, at the Grammar School, which was directly across in front of our house.

11.

Sanford, Florida, October 26, 1953

Grammar School
Plans Halloween

The Sanford Grammar School announced today that the Halloween treat for the school children on Friday will consist of free ice Cream with their lunch.

In the afternoon, Harry Wise, a magician, will give a free show.

Friday, October 30, 1953 THE SANFORD HERALD

The first two promotional advertisements of Harry Wise. He was only 18 years old when he first appeared in the press as a magician.

[Courtesy Sanford Herald]

I left my house, walked across to the school and upstairs to the auditorium. I did my show for those kids, about forty minutes, then packed up and went downstairs and the principal paid me twenty-five dollars. Think of that, in 1953 that was a lot of money! I knew right then, this is it, this is what I'm going to do.

"When I got back to the house, Dad told me about a magician, Art Burris was his name, that was going to be at the Halloween carnival over at Westside School. So, that evening after supper, I walked the three blocks over to Westside School where I met Art Burris, who I would know for the next twenty-years...he was a big influence on my life. But the man in town who helped me was Bill Hoffman, and also Mr. Harris who was the Ritz Theater manager in 1953. He was the one who introduced me to Bill Hoffman. Now Bill Hoffman had a radio repair shop in town, next to the Ritz Theater, but in the twenties and thirties he had a big magic show of his own. I still got one of his props that was built in 1927 at Cowen's machine shop. Hoffman was a heavy hitter, he was the RCA projector repairman for the entire state of Florida and the Florida State Theater Corporation. Bill Hoffman taught me several things and I still do a cut-and-restored rope routine that he taught me in 1953. It's fifty years later and I still do that at every show.

"Now things were moving fast, I did the show at the Grammar School; I met Art Burris the same night at the Westside Halloween carnival, and the very next night, Halloween night, October 31, 1953, I was playing the stage at the Ritz. Now keep in mind that I was only eighteen and it had been my plan all along, to turn pro when I was eighteen...I was just short of my nineteenth birthday. This was a midnight show at the Ritz and we packed the house, but everybody knew me. October 30th and 31st, were the two most favorable days in my entire life. I actually launched my profession on Halloween night in 1953.

"Art Burris brought over some magicians from Orlando to see my show, and Burling Volta Hull came over to see it. I first met Burling Hull in 1952, he had been the *White Wizard* in Vaudeville back in the twenties...I mean he was a big timer. When Vaudeville was big, he was big. He was the first man to do magic on CBS television out of New York, but by this time he was retired and living in Deland, Florida. He was truly the Edison of modern magic...he wrote more books and invented more tricks than anybody in the business. I spent sixty-eight cents to ride the Greyhound bus to Deland to spend the afternoon with him, and another sixty-eight cents to ride the bus back home. People today wouldn't believe that you could ride the bus for sixty-eight cents.

"Now Art Burris was my friend for twenty years and another moving force in my life. He had played Vaudeville, CCC camps, and theaters, and could tell you all kinds of things. He was a walking book on entertainment.

"I was getting the Billboard newspaper, now that was the main show business paper. It costs 35 cents and the lady that ran the news stand downtown in the bank building...she'd get one every Thursday for me and put my name on it. I'd go get it that afternoon when Dad and I came back from work.

"In the early fifties, whenever a ghost show played through town...like Doctor Silkini, Chan Loo's 'Horrors of the Orient'...Bill Brundell with his 'Shock'...I'd go meet them and talk to them and then go out and get my buddies...like Lynn Ashe...and all...to help them on stage. When the showmen hit this town they didn't know it...but they had a little stock company of stooges ready and waiting for them.

"I never had formal training, that's what makes *David Copperfield* so great, he took formal acting training, dance, and all that. I was just ordering stuff from comic books and doing magic and flying-by-the-seat-of-my-pants one hundred percent. Johnny Cates, who I'll talk about later...was the one that really taught me stage craft, makeup, mike technique, how to bow, how to get applause...or ask for it nicely. But even without a formal start, I really did have the largest magic and illusion show in the Southeast and I did have many outlets in my career, like circuses, the mentalist routine, clowning and all. So I've been more diversified than some of the others.

"In 1955 there was a magician appearing on Orlando television, on Channel 6, nobody remembers him...he was a wonderful gentleman named *Andy Youngman*. He was from Melbourne, Florida, and always kidded everybody that he was the only 'young man' in the phone book. He was billed as the "*White Mahatma*" on *Uncle Walt's Adventures*.

"I drove over to Orlando to meet the man, to talk with him and all. I guess I made about three or four visits with him at the studio and he led me to my next gig. Now in '55, Jax Southern Liquor Company ran a campaign for *Old Stag*. It was a national promotion campaign, but Jax Liquors handled it in Florida.

14.

"That was in March and April '55, and the man that handled the Old Stag promotion had come down to Jacksonville because he had heard about Andy Youngman. He called Andy and offered him the job playing 'Mr. Old Stag.' Andy thought it over a day or two, but he had an eye problem, and when he found out that he had to wear an eight-and-a-half foot tall, fur suit with antlers, he knew he couldn't handle it. He was already in his sixties and he knew he couldn't handle it.

"Now here's the rest of the story. I was still painting houses, and yes, I was doing a carnival date or two and birthday parties and all that. One morning, my dad and I were loading the car to go paint houses, and Mr. Owens steps out the back of his Westside Grocery Store...our back yard came right up to the back of the Westside Grocery store. Anyway, Mr. Owens steps out and says, 'Harry you're wanted on the phone, some man in Orlando wants to talk to you about a job.' Now we didn't have a phone at home at this time. We had one off and on since '43, but Dad got mad at the phone company and had disconnected the phone right as I, the 'El Great One,' was launching my career. Anyhow...I get on the line with this man...I'm in the grocery store with my paint clothes on, and the man says please come to Orlando and see me at the Angelbilt hotel. He told me that he had offered the job to Andy Youngman and that it was a big promotion for Old Stag, and that Andy turned it down but told the man that I would do it. I said, 'Well, I don't know, tell me about it.' Then I asked him how he knew to call me at a grocery store in the backyard of my house. He said it was a phone operator in Sanford named Violet. Well this was Violet Spivey and she had been a school mate of mine. She knew where I lived and knew the Westside Grocery was next door to our house. So, Violet Spivey had put me in contact with this man, and it was Andy Youngman who had recommended me for the job.

"I quickly changed my clothes and drove over to Orlando to meet with the man and we signed a deal and that's when I became Mr. Old Stag. I toured all over the state, doing bars, night clubs, parades, you name it. A hundred and fifty dollars a week, all restaurants and motels paid for and they furnished me a jeep to drive. That's right...a jeep fixed-up with Old Stag advertising. So I became Mr. Old Stag thanks to Violet Spivey, a telephone operator, and my magical friend, Andy Youngman. It wasn't a big gig because it only lasted a couple of months.

"As Mr. Old Stag, I went all over Central Florida in that suit,

15.

Harry Wise as "Mr. Old Stag." [*Wise collection*]

from Leesburg to Mount Dora and Orlando. I was even right downtown in Sanford on First street, standing around as Mr. Old Stag in front of the Town Pump, while the liquor salesman was inside selling liquor and beer and stuff. I was just outside on the sidewalk waving at cars...when up comes Henry Russell's wife, Eleanor, and she looks me up and down. I'm looking at her through this little ol' window thing in the stag head and she says, 'My god you're outlandish!' I said, 'But you know me, I'm your neighbor.' She says, 'My heavens! Harry Wise! I'd know that voice anywhere.'

"The Mr. Old Stag thing was a lark. Now as Mr. Old Stag, I did magic in bars and night clubs, but I had to take off the head piece otherwise I couldn't see what I was doing.

"I almost got into trouble in Leesburg when I crashed a parade. I didn't think anything of it, but we get into town and there was this parade in progress and...the liquor salesman says, 'You ought to run out there and get in it. Put that head piece on and run out there in the parade.' I said, 'Heck no we'll get in trouble!' He says, 'Just do it...I'll follow along in the car and when I toot the horn, you just jump in and we'll take off.' So...ha, I'm in the parade just boppin' along...there's thousands of people watching the procession...and I'm skipping along, waving...and all that...and kids are running up wanting to hold Mr. Old Stag's hand. But two or three mothers got irate because Mr. Old Stag was the embodiment of a liquor promotion. Now I didn't put that together in my head...I was just out there in the parade having fun. Now the salesman knew the town well-enough to go around and get ahead of the parade...so, near the end, I jumped in the car and we take off out to the edge of town to get a cold drink. Sure 'nuff the police was looking for us because we should not have been in that damn parade with a liquor ad. That salesman had to know this, but he feigned total innocence, he was a liquor salesman this was what he did for a living and I've always been convinced that he knew we weren't suppose to be in that parade. Anyway, I was young and so-called naïve...which is just another word for stupidity. All together I was in three parades as Old Mr. Stag...two with permission and one as an outlaw.

17.

Advertisements for Chan Loo's ghost shows that Harry Wise remembers attending as a boy at the Ritz theater. [Wise collection]

Chapter 3

"The only uniform I wanted to wear was a tux and tails, a cape and top hat."
Harry Wise 1957

"In '57 a ghost show played here in town...at the Ritz theater...and I went down to see them. That was March '57, and I heard that the whole troupe was staying in the Montezuma Hotel...so here I marched into the Montezuma Hotel...up to the desk...I forget the man's name...but I said point me to the rooms that the show troupe's got. He said go down the hall...upstairs, two doors on the right...or whatever. Anyway, I knocked on the door...and it was Johnny Cates out of Houston, Texas, that had the ghost show. So we meet and talk for awhile, then he said let's go get a meal over at the Sanford Restaurant, which was right near the theater. It hadn't been twenty minutes after knocking on his door that I was having supper with him. He wanted me to go with them right then, but I couldn't because I had just been drafted to go into the army. It's a long story about all that...my army career was un-illustrious. But Johnny Cates put on a grand show at the Ritz that night. I followed them over to Orlando when they played the Rialto theater on Church street. Johnny and I kept in contact and were always calling or writing to each other during the time I was in the army.

"I used to make a joke about the draft. I always said, 'Dammit I'm going to let them draft me, I'm not going to volunteer, they can come and get me...but I don't want to get in that draft because I'll catch a cold and get pneumonia!' That's exactly what happened, they drafted me and processed me at Fort Jackson, South Carolina and I ended up confined to the hospital with pneumonia and a 102 temperature. That was because they ran us through showers that were ice cold. Well that put me behind the rest of the guys in my group. But I shouldn't have been inducted because back in 1948 I had broken my leg in three places and Doctor W. D. Walker operated on this leg and put three pins in it. The army was not supposed to take me and Doctor W. D. Walker furnished me with x-rays and said don't worry the army won't take me. They horse'd me back and forth to Jacksonville twice and the third time they inducted me into the army. Three times they did this...well I knew I didn't want to be in the army.

"After I got out of the hospital at Fort Jackson, they shipped me down to Fort Gorden, Georgia, outside of Augusta, for basic training there. Now I told the world since I was fifteen that the only uniform that I wanted to wear was a tux and tails, a cape and a top hat...in basic training if you go walking out in tails, cape and a top hat...you're going to be put somewhere. Now there was no way I could take a ninety pound pack on this leg with three pins in it. Anyhow, in the army they horse'd me around and gave me whirlpool treatments and all that. Then I met a wonderful gentleman, a sergeant. I was in Company C, and right next door was Company D, and he was in that company. We met by accident and started going to lunch together and to the P.X. I still remember him, his name was Sergeant Sanford, just like the name of my home town. He wasn't a showman...he was a career army man and after I got out of the army we wrote cards and letters back and forth...but we never saw one another again.

"In the army I got a weekend pass to go into Augusta even though I was confined to quarters pending discharge by now. Anyway, I got a special pass, although the company commander didn't want to issue it. One of my buddies named Boykin went to him and said, 'Look...the circus is in town and Wise has to go over there...he has people on the circus.' Well, no I didn't...but I wanted to go to that circus and it was Boykin that got me the damn pass.

"I went down to that beautiful Bell Auditorium in Augusta and saw the Polack Brothers' circus. There was a dog act on this show...it was Angela Wilnow and her Braves, a magnificent act featuring trained collies. This was the first circus act that I really fell in love with. I was young, and so smitten with this beautiful woman that I went out back of the auditorium and

20.

found her trailer and knocked on the door so I could meet her. She talked with me, a little condescending, but nice. She played all the big dates, even the Ed Sullivan show. Little did I know at the time, our paths would again cross many years later. Well...to make a long story short, that was a wonderful, charming day for me. A couple of weeks go by and I'm still not discharged from the army, and the Fair is opening in Augusta, I think it was the World of Mirth midway. I knew there would be a magician on the sideshow but I didn't know who.

"I got a pass for the weekend and went to the Fair, and sure enough, there was a magician, named Roy...Roy LeRoy...and his daughter was one of the girl show dancers. She was lovely...I fell in love with the magician's daughter...but she was busy and I was very young and overly-impressed with the world and didn't even meet her. Roy was such a wonderful man to me during the couple of days I visited the Fair. I'll never forget him, but we never saw each other again.

"I did have a little show adventure in the army. My mother and dad sent me my show to the base and ah...I was furnished a special cabinet to lock it in because I was afraid those guys were going to steal my silks, props....but nobody ever touched a thing. I did one show on Fort Gordon in an auditorium there for the guys.

"It was December 13th, 1957, ...Friday the 13th, when I finally got out of the Army and got back to Sanford. I ate dinner and jumped in my car and drove over to Orlando to see Art Burris. I got to his house and his mother was there, she was in her seventies then...and she says, 'Harry I think you will find my son just down Colonial Drive at the Mickey Mouse tavern. He thinks I don't know that he goes in there and has a beer.' She's in her seventies and he's in his fifties and he's sneaking around to have a beer. So...I go down there and sure enough Art is having a beer. I walked in and he couldn't believe it was me. So...we promptly get in my car and drive over to Lake Eola that night where they had just opened that new rainbow fountain in the middle of the lake. We sat there about two hours on that chilly night, just talking and having a ball and being buddies...I'll never forget that night with Art Burris. He was the first man I went to see after getting out of the army.

"I had met Dave Madden back in 1955, you know he played Rueben on the *Partridge Family*, and Earl the basketball coach on *Alice*...anyway Dave was playing a club in Orlando in December so I went to see him a few times. So, I finished out the year visiting friends...Dave and I still keep in contact. He's retired to Miami now.

"In March I got a wire from Houston...from Johnny Cates, wanting me to come out to Texas. I caught the Greyhound bus and went out to Houston and joined him. We rehearsed a couple of days in his backyard. I knew I liked him from the year before when I met him in Sanford. Johnny had a Chevrolet panel truck that we had the show in. We did a six minute opening using doves and all...then the rest was a fast-moving, hell's a-poppin' type show. Johnny had a beautiful black and white Buick sedan and when we left Houston to open the show, this was March, we left together in his car and the other assistant, and the girl on the show, followed in the truck.

"I'll never forget what Johnny Cates said to me, I knew we had perfect simpatico, and Johnny said, 'Harry we're going to open in Sapulpa, Oklahoma. The first show, or two, might go a little rough, but after that we'll have it all smoothed out and I'll tell you this, you've come all the way from Florida to join me, and if we don't make but a nickel you've got half of it son because you mean business.' I'll never forget that. We were close friends for the rest of his life...unfortunately he died in 1984 at the Texas Association of Magicians convention. He made the whole convention, but that night when he was leaving with his wife, Margie, he fell dead of a heart attack in his motel room. I knew him all those years... he's the one who taught me stage craft. When I first saw him at the Ritz he was magnificent, his voice, mannerism, stage presence, and all...he had a magnetic personality.

"I didn't have formal training, I was brash, I just went out on stage and did it...because I loved it. I remember Dave Madden and Volta Hull saying, 'Harry, just remember they are paying to see you, you're not paying to see them.' When you think about it, that's a stabilizing thought. The magic they do today ain't the same...half of it is electronics...there's no assistant in the wings with wax to add to something...or with a load, an animal load slung, or a thread going across the stage. Now there's just some technician punching a button on something. That's not stage craft, we've lost the art of stage entertainment. I don't like that kind of magic, I want manually brought about magic and illusions. It's the difference between being a chef or preparing a TV dinner in a microwave, I want to be the chef.

"We opened in Sapulpa, Oklahoma, I played Frankenstein every night, and in addition to that...I assisted Johnny on the

Ghostmaster Johnny Cates on stage [Showtime archives]

opening. I was the guy who put Johnny's wife on the decapitation table so he could chop her head off. I was also the stage manager...now get this...*stage manager.* I drove the truck; made sure the dry cleaning was done every Monday morning in whatever town we were in and kept the birds clean, once or twice a day everyday. I made sure the truck was oiled and gassed-up and that the tires were good and all that. I had to unload and setup the show and make sure all the gaffs and gimmicks were alright and the electric was setup right, and that the mike worked and the music worked. Then I had to go up stairs to the projectionist and give the cues for the blackout. We tried to open the show with a spotlight if the theater had one, so I'd give the projectionist the spotlight cues and stage cues. Sometimes we had a theater with footlights and all.

"Every morning I had to mail the film trailer to the next theater we were playing. That's like a preview shown on the screen advertising coming attractions. We were running film trailers two weeks in advance promoting the show. We had forty-six trailers. Sometimes we had to send several to the next town if they had more than one theater and a drive-in movie where they could cross-plug the show. Now these film trailers had a date strip that had to be changed. The theater manager would take off the old date strip and put on the new date. They'd use banana oil, or glue...or whatever to splice the date strip to the film. The forty-by-sixty banners for advertising the show came in direct from the printer, usually National Poster or Globe, all that was ordered a month in advance. We used posters, flyers, radio tape, and all...these expenses came off the top when we settled with the theater after the show. There was no guarantee on the ghost show, it was a straight split after expenses.

"We're still in '58, doing some Oklahoma and Texas dates, all movie theaters. Johnny always said that we were killing the last rung on the ladder of vaudeville. We had people that came to us and said our show was the last to play because they were tearing down the theater...that it was being replaced by a parking lot or a new bank. some of those theaters had been there 46 years...and we were the last stage show to play them. I wasn't listening to what was being said at the time, 'cause I didn't realize that in just ten years there would be no theaters to put a ghost show in...movie theaters today do not have stages...there are hardly any of the small theaters, the vaudeville-type houses left in the United States. You used to go into a town, walk in to an independent theater and spend twenty minutes with the manager and set the date. You could book these theaters yourself.

"We were doing six and seven days a week with the Cates show, sometimes two shows a night, seven and nine, and sometimes a midnight show. We worked all over the United States. I always played the Frankenstein monster and was the guy who pretended to lose the snake in the audience. I'd be backstage, behind the curtain, and I'd start hollering and Johnny would be out front yelling to me, 'What's the matter Harry, what's goin' on back there?.' I'd yell back, 'Oh god the snakes are loose, the snakes are loose!.' He'd yell, 'What?' Then I'd come running out with a rubber snake...and in those days I'd actually leap into the audience and head up the aisle with it...and right then they'd hit the blackout! While the lights were out, I'd roll the snake up you see, and stuff it in my cummerbund. Lights would come back on, and Johnny would say, 'Where's the snake? Then I'd say, 'I lost it! I lost it!...there it is going under the first row of seats!' Man, everybody would go crazy, the girls would be screaming, 'cause they thought I'd lost that snake. Later in my own show I used a different plan.

24.

I didn't send anybody out there in the audience with the snake, I'd do a throw with it. The assistant would be yelling that the snakes are loose, and I would say, 'Well do something! Do something!' And He'd come running out swinging the snake around, and I'd say, 'What are you doing? Are you insane?' On the third swing we'd hit the blackout and he'd throw the snake back into the wing. And then when the lights came back on, I'd say, 'You didn't throw that snake in the audience did you?' 'Well yes I did...you said to do something.' Then he'd look down and point, 'My god there it goes under the first row, see it, there it goes.' I mean that would just panic the whole audience, it was a strong bit.

"In Illinois, outside of Flora, which I later played with the *Franzen circus*, well...we were making a jump with the Cates show, trying to get to Springfield, and I tried to pass two pickup trucks and ah, well...I didn't make it. I had to hit the shoulder of the road because a car was coming toward me. And when I hit that shoulder the show truck flipped and ended-up in a ditch. And the show truck is exactly like this...on its side, and I'm down here on the driver's side looking into the ditch, and I hear cows mooing over here above me. There was no water in the ditch and I'm next to somebody's farm. I did cut the ignition off...but the doves and wardrobe was on top of me. I mean the whole dove cage ripped lose and I'm down under there feeling myself...I knew it was bad...but I wasn't hurt! I narrowly escaped death on that one. The cars and trucks on the highway just kept going by. So, here I am laying there...my hands still on the steering wheel...and I hear footsteps on the side of the truck. Yes...I hear footsteps! Well, the windows were opened and this man saw the mess and jumps down on the side of the truck and walks his way up to the front... to the cab. He looks down at me, and I look up at him, and he says, 'Mister, my name is Hand, Clarence Hand, can I give you a hand?' And he reaches down and pulls me up...out through the window of that truck! I'll never forget it, can you imagine such a thing? That man's name was 'Hand' and he says, 'Can I give you a hand?'

"That man took me to a gas station. It's about two o'clock in the afternoon, and keep in mind, we got a seven and nine o'clock show to do. I had the number to the theater so I called it. Johnny was in the Buick up ahead of me. So when he gets to the theater the manager tells him, 'You gotta go back and getcha buddy; he's back there in a wrecked truck just out of

25.

Flora there. Johnny comes back and we get a wrecker and get it up on the highway. Johnny says, 'Harry we got to get to that theater; we can't break that contract, we got to get there! The whole front end of the truck is messed up. We finally get to the theater, an hour late...but we unload and get set up and do a show that night. I can't remember the name of that theater. The next morning I'm up getting that truck fixed, it cost a couple hundred bucks and we were back on the road.

"We played several big houses, the Temple Theater in Tampa, a real showcase house. My favorite was the State Theater in Schenectady, a couple thousand-seat house. The biggest with Johnny was the wonderful Sanger Theater in New Orleans, it was the pilot house for the Paramount-Gulf Theater Corporation. It had beautiful crystal chandeliers in the lobby and you get your ticket and go in, and go upstairs, and they'd give you a glass of champagne. You talk about a top date...I played it with Johnny and repeated it after I got my own ghost show in 1965.

"We get into Canada, this was in 1958, Ontario...I think it was Owens Sound, and we pulled up with the truck right in the back of the theater and unloaded right into the backstage. As we were coming in, I had spotted an ice cream shop across the street...or alley, up front on the main street. I told Johnny, 'I'm going to go get me an ice cream' and he said, 'Well I'll go get our rooms and check in.' So after we get everything set up, I go out the front of the theater to get my ice cream and I looked down this alley behind the theater...and here's ten or twelve kids back there...one of them is up on the roof of a garage...and four or five up in a tree. So I go back there to talk with those kids...I figured they didn't see us unload and wouldn't know me. I said, 'Kids what are you doing here? What in the world is all this back here in this alley?' And they said, 'Oh there's a monster! There's a monster show playing here tonight and there's a monster in that theater! We saw somebody taking all kinds of stuff in there.'

"I said, 'You saw a monster!' I could tell they were already crazy with anticipation and imagination. So I says, 'You boys wanna be careful 'cause if there's a monster in that theater...there could be snakes too...and no telling what else!'

"Then I go back up and talked with the manager for a little bit. I come back out and go over and get another ice cream cone. By now there's thirty kids or so back there. And I go back and talk to them again. I said, 'What in the world!' They said,

'Oh we're waiting.' One of them had a stick and a couple had rocks...they were going to get that monster. I'm serious. So, I went back inside the theater and got into that Frankenstein getup and I start banging on that back exit from the inside...hittin' the door...kicking it with them big heavy shoes. I'm making noise, growlin' and kicking that door...then I threw the slide bar and kept shaking the door until it went wide open. I'm standing there framed in that door...then I leaped out and just stood there growling. Those kids went every direction...nobody threw a rock, nobody tried to hit me with a stick...they were screaming and running everywhere. By now I'm wanting another ice cream. I go back inside and get everything laid out and put on my street clothes and go out the front of the theater...and honest...there had to be fifty or sixty kids that had gathered back there. I went back there again and said, 'What's going on here? They said, 'Oh mister, you ain't going to believe us...everyone of us saw him...a big ol' green-headed monster came out of that door...came out right there...right there!' Talk about funny, I never will forget those kids. I've never seen such exuberance. But the word got out quick and we packed the house that night.

"We were doing a show in 1959 in Sedalia, Missouri, and I went to the theater manager and told him that I needed a sharp young man sixteen, seventeen or eighteen, to rehearse two or three bits backstage for the show...and the rest of them we'll work cold on the hypnotic bits...in other words we'd just pick them out of the audience...but we needed this one to rehearse the act with us. The manager said, 'Go down and talk to the leader of the motorcycle gang, a boy named Johnny. He's a smart aleck but he's handsome, the local ladies' man and he's straight.' I said, 'What? The head of the motorcycle gang?' And he said, 'He don't drink, he don't do dope, he just likes his five or six buddies and his motorcycle. Go talk to him.'

"So I went down there and talked to him and we hit it off just like that. Well, here we had the local motorcycle guy backstage to be our stooge in the hypnotic bit...making love to the coat or broomstick. Some times we would do the pants pulling...where Johnny Cates would pull the pants off the kid. That took a stooge to be in special pants held together with Velcro or whatever. We used this motorcycle guy for that stunt, pulled his pants off and he goes running off stage with those silly looking polka-dotted drawers on. He knew he was going to make everybody in town laugh...that's what appealed to him.

Thousands of Central Floridians who were kids in the early 1960s still remember Harry Wise as television's Mr. Magic.

Chapter 4

"Wise the Wizard, Florida Television's Mr. Magic."
WDBO TV, 1959

"I got back home in '59, we had come out of Canada...and went back to Houston and I got the bus back to Florida. I went back to painting houses for the time being. I got in touch with my friend Lynn Ashe, we'd been friends since 1951 and by '59 he had done a few magic shows with me and eventually became my stage manager.

"Anyway, in October '59, Lynn and I dressed-up on Halloween night. I made-up like Frankenstein and we sat on the front porch of the house...and about six-thirty in the evening, the kids started coming trick-or-treating, oh...there must have been forty or fifty that year. I was sittin' between the front steps and my mother, who was on the end of the porch with the candy...and those tricker treaters wouldn't pass Frankenstein to get their treats. Talk about word spreading fast...we had at least fifty kids or so that night. All Frankenstein had to do was growl and those kids would scatter.

"There was a Halloween carnival going on over at Southside School...and I told Lynn come on back here with me and I'll fix you up as the Hunchback. I had a special coat...and shoved a pillow up the back...and a mask and all. I dubbed the hunchback *'Haster the Unspeakable'*...which is an H. P. Lovecraft character from his writings. I made myself up as Frankenstein. I had a beautiful Kaiser, I had painted it black, a four door sedan, and we drove over to the carnival and it was full of people. Well...we parked the car and walked across the street right into the middle of that carnival and a hundred kids dropped what they were doing, stopped playing games and all...and they're all running along and talking and laughing with the monster and holding his hand. Not a one of them was a smart aleck...they just wanted to hold the monster's hand...and to talk to him. Then this woman comes up and puts something in my pocket. I felt her hand in my pocket...and she says to me, 'This is my phone number mister...I want you to call me tomorrow. I want to do a story on you.' We stole the carnival that night, I couldn't believe it...we were like the Pied Piper with all those kids tagging along after us.

"So the next day I called that lady and went out to see her and we sat in her kitchen sipping coffee while she asked me questions and started writing. About four or five weeks later, in December, it came out as a feature story in the Orlando Sentinel...with a banner headline...'*Frankenstein Magician Visits Home In Sanford.*' They ran a picture of me and beside it was a picture of me dressed as the monster. What a story it was, it told all about me being on the road with Johnny Cates, doing magic and all...she was just a good writer.

"In the meantime, while waiting for that story to come out, I went over to Orlando to visit the '*White Mahatma*,' Andy Youngman, again. He was still on Uncle Walt's Adventures on Channel Six, once or twice a month. Well, he comes out of the studio and says, 'Harry why don't you take this over for me?' And I said, 'What...?' And he says, 'Why don't you come be the magician on this show. I'm near seventy and not feeling too good and it's just getting to me.. the driving over here and all.'

"So the next day I called Walter E. Sickles...he was *Uncle Walt*...now he was also the program director for Cherry Broadcasting, which was WDBO Television in those days. Now...it's December '59, you see, and I make an appointment in January, about the fourth or fifth, to go over to the office. So the day comes for the appointment and I go over there and walk into Uncle Walt's office and we hit it off pretty good. He asked me if I had anything with me so I could do some magic. Well...I had my special table and props out in the car and he told me to bring it all in and set it up in the lobby. He said, 'I'm going to get Colin Murchison to watch this. I said to myself 'Oh, lord,' because there's more to this story about Colin, he was the stage manager. This gets retroactive in a moment so stay with me. Anyhow, I get all set up in the lobby and I do the salt vanish using Walt's handkerchief. They were impressed with that one, so I do the milk pitcher thing, cut and restored rope,

30.

about ten or twelve minutes of tricks for them. Walt looks at Colin Murchison and says, 'Colin what do you say we put him on? Andy told me we might be talking to this young man. We'll just call him 'Mr. Magic.' Colin tells Walt, 'He looks good to me too Walt.' So it was Walter Sickles that first came up with the name Mr. Magic that I used for many years.

"Now what nobody remembered that day...was something that happened back in 1957. Channel Six had put an ad in the paper wanting acts to come audition for a local talent show. So, I went over and auditioned and Colin Murchison was the man that turned me down! And this was the very same man in 1960 who told Walt Sickles, 'He looks good to me too, Walt.' Now Colin and I became good friends after that but he never put it together that I was the one he had turned down for that damn talent show three years before.

"I went on television for the first time on January 19th 1960, on *Uncle Walt's Adventures* as Mr. Magic. Thanks to Andy Youngman I became a household name for every kid in Central Florida. Everyday at five o'clock they'd be glued to the TV watching Uncle Walt and Mr. Magic. In printing I started using '*Wise the Wizard, Florida Television's Mr. Magic.*'

"In late February and March, I was playing those big shopping centers in Melbourne and Cocoa with Walt. They brought him in as a personality. You know...they ran ads like, '*Hey Kids Come See Uncle Walt and Mr. Magic in person*,' that sort of thing, which was good for me. The TV exposure started getting me all kinds of tie-ins and bookings, birthday parties...all of a sudden all kinds of things started happening.

"Orlando television was wonderful, and I did it all live. In those days I had some nice props, shiny dove pans, rice bowls and all, all chrome, and they had a special stuff they'd spray on to dull them down because it would glare too much in the camera. They'd always ask me when I went in to do a show, 'You got any of those shiny props that we need to dull down?'

"We also had a live audience in the studio...the bleachers, the peanut gallery where the kids sat. The sponsors were *Tarnow, down-on-the-farm* meat products, *T. G. Lee Dairy, Royal Castle Birch Beer,* and *Kentucky Fried Chicken.* Often times I would stop at Royal Castle on my way over and pickup the Birch Beer for the kids on the show. Birch Beer was a good beverage, very much like root beer. For four or five years I did the T. G. Lee Dairy employees' annual Christmas party. I did several company picnics during this time.

31.

"Beginning in 1961, for three years in a row, I did an annual employees' picnic for an Orlando company. I did it on the back of a lumber truck but had to do two separate shows. I did a show on one side of the park for the white employees, then had to pack-up and drive all the way across the park to the other side and do the same show for the black employees.

I was on television, technically, from 1960 to March 16, 1965. But by 1963 I'm in and out of Georgia, Mississippi and Alabama doing shows for FRS...*Fund Raising Services.* That took me throughout the Southeast doing a special promotion called *Auction Dollar Days.* This was a promotion thing for local merchants everywhere from Umatilla, Florida, Lake City, to Greenville, Alabama, Tennessee, Bowling Green, Kentucky, and towns like that. A lot of times I couldn't be on T.V. because I would be on the road...so I'd call Walt and he'd tell me when to come in...usually about twice a week when I was in town.

"When I was doing Auction Dollar Days, I just did the magic show as the attraction to draw the people...then they would hold an auction with these auction dollars that were donated by the merchants in town that people could use to buy things with. I never was the auctioneer, that was usually the dime store manager, shoe store owner...or somebody like that.

"I was all over the place with Auction Dollar Days...it was quite a promotion for merchants and it kept me busy from Florida to Kentucky. I guess I entertained many thousands at those Auction Dollar Days.

"In London, Kentucky, there was a good hotdog place, it was the pool hall but they had the freshest buns and the best tasting wieners For years when I was going back and forth through Kentucky, I'd stop and get a hotdog, or two, or three, depending on how hungry I was. When I was up there doing Auction Dollar Days in October '63 I stopped there and got myself a hotdog. Well...when I left the billiard parlor it was getting dark but I just decided to drive around town and see some of the neighborhoods. Anyway, I'm driving around enjoying looking at the town and all of a sudden the front end of the car falls out from under me. It was my station wagon, in the back was my wardrobe, my birds and all, and my car is like this...just teetering on the edge of a cliff. The road just ended right there! A twenty-foot drop; no sign or nothing! I'm looking down into somebody's kitchen and they're sitting in there having dinner. I opened the car door real easy...and the people get up from their dinner and walk outside and look up at me. I'm saying, 'What is this? There's no sign or nothing, I was just ridin' around and came off the end of the road.' The man looks up and says, 'Oh that happens all the time. The funeral parlor is right behind you, go talk to that man, he'll get you a wrecker.' I go knock on the funeral parlor door and the guy comes out laughing, 'Yeah I heard it, this happens all the time, somebody's always running off there.' I said, 'Where's the signs? Where's the barrier? He said, 'Oh the city won't put nothing up...let me call Joe and he'll come get you out.' He called a wrecker for me and it came out and hooked up to the back and pulled me off there for five dollars.' It might sound funny now but it wasn't back then. That was in London, Kentucky...I never will forget that one.

"In Bainbridge, Georgia, in 1963 just before I segued into my own ghost show tour...I played the Auction Dollar Days for the Bainbridge Merchants Association. We did the show at a wonderful place, it was the bandstand in a park. Well, everything is set up for the auction and I'm on center stage doing the magic and it comes time for my guillotine routine. I had it covered with a striped cloth. I asked for a volunteer and this little black kid, about ten years old, comes up to help me. I proceed to tell him that he has to be brave...and that you have to be courageous...and all that. He says, 'Yes sir, I am.' So I tell him to watch me, and I go over and uncover the guillotine. He took one look at it, he looked at me and looked at it. I took the top off and said to him, 'Now young man, I want you to get down on your knees and place your head right in here in this neck section.' He took off running...leaped clean over the wall...and kept on running until he was out of sight. Everybody, five hundred or so, were laughing. We watched him running until he was out of sight...I don't think they've seen him since. The Merchants Association president came to me and said, 'That was the funniest thing I ever saw...how'd you get that boy to do that?' I said, 'I didn't get that boy to do that, that was natural, he just took off running when he saw that guillotine. He took one look at that thing and took off.' Well all you can do is keep the show going...but after that every kid out there had their arm up wanting to come up for the guillotine routine.

Top Photo.
Harry Wise amazing a crowd at one of his many Auction Dollar Days magic shows.

Left Photo.
The infamous guillotine that Harry Wise used to "chop the heads off" thousands of his fans. For years, this illusion was a main attraction on Dr. Jekyl's Weird Show.

Chapter 5

"Coast to Coast with the Ghost Show"

"Now it was in 1963 when I got into my own ghost show. It was a lark because I was both producer and presenter of the show. I had been framing the ghost show in my backyard ever since 1959 when I got off the Johnny Cates show. My buddy, Don Masters, sketched-out spiders, big skulls, and bats, and groping hands, eyes, and he'd put them on roll-up window shades. I was always painting something luminous in the backyard so I'd been working on my ghost show three or four years. I built a couple of props, like a head burning illusion, things like that. I had all my notes made…and I knew I could front it, after being with Johnny Cates, there was no doubt about that.

"I once asked Bill Brundell, now he was a fine Florida showman, 'How do you make a living with a magic show and a ghost show, and everything you're doing and all. Are you making any money? I had known Brundell since '52 when he had his *"Temple of Mystery"* show. I said, 'Tell me what your secret is.' He said, 'Well Harry, when you make twenty cents, you live on twenty cents, and when you make two-hundred dollars, you live on twenty cents.' That's what Bill Brundell told me.. ha, ha. He later took out a show called *"Brundell Presents Shock."* One time he played the Ritz and as a promotion, did a blindfold drive in a car around the block here in town. He had two beautiful skeleton tables that he used on his show. I ended up with those tables, they're antiques now but I have used them many times on my show.

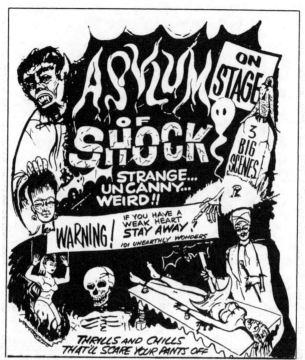

A show poster for Bill Brundell's Asylum of Shock
[Author's collection]

"Lynn Ashe was working for the grocery store downtown and I said to him, 'Lynn, stop this foolishness for thirty-six dollars a week and go on the road with me.' Lynn had already helped me with local magic shows in school auditoriums. I said, 'Get serious about this thing and go on the road with me...I'll pay you a hundred and a half a week to be my right hand man...my stage manager.' The next day Lynn quit his job at the grocery store and we started rehearsing in the backyard. We tacked up a cue sheet on the side of the house and we'd rehearse right there in the backyard.

"Now, when you have luminous ghosts, rubber snakes that look just like real moccasins, a theater blackout, monsters that come out and grab girls out of the audience, well...that's a real ghost show. We didn't just do fifty minutes of magic with a blackout...buddy, we did a real show...six minutes of magic, three blackouts, the hypnotic bits, lose the snake routine, the Mummy, Frankenstein, the Hunchback and all that. We had all the routines, the hot seat boy, pull-the-boy's-shorts-off...and then cut his head off with the guillotine for the finale.

"The show was titled *Dr. Jekyl and his Weird Show*. When we first started out we actually used stooges, we'd take them backstage to rehearse...but that got to be such a bore and a chore that we started working them cold. Johnny Cates first started that on his show. We would just go out in the audience and pick them out, and as you're walking down the aisle with them you tell them just do everything the man tells you; just fall in with the show and help us make these people laugh. Now when you say that to them, you'll very seldom have a smart aleck...and a smart aleck will always be a boy. Most of the girls didn't give us any problems.

"We did several hypnosis routines, the hot seat, where the boy would be hypnotized and he'd squirm around and jump up from his seat like it was hot. Another hypnotic routine was where we would give a boy a broom, or a coat, and tell him it was a girl and he would caress it and love it. But here's the secret behind these routines. There was so much heat from the American Medical Association in the fifties and sixties about hypnotists...that we did what is called a pseudo-hypnotic act, it was an act not real hypnotism. However, both Johnny Cates and I could do it, we never did real hypnotism on stage.

"We usually had three or four people on the ghost show...usually three...and we'd always get a local boy to do one of the monsters, either the Mummy or Frankenstein, 'cause I couldn't do it because I was fronting the show at that time as the mad Doctor Jekyl. To get a boy to work with us, we'd ask the theater manager if he knew somebody...or go to the local billiard parlor and get one. There was always some kid around that was willing to work or just be in the show. In Steubenville, Ohio, I asked the manager about a couple of boys and he sent me down to the local pool hall. That's where I got my Frankenstein in Steubenville...in the very pool hall where Dean Martin had once played pool...you know that Steubenville was his hometown.

"Now, in 1963, Lynn Ashe took on the name "Lynn Strange." I loved the name Lynn Strange...it was perfect and on stage it sounded good. Now speaking of names, right after the magic opening, I did what Johnny Cates used to do. I'd introduce my girl and boy assistants...I always had a fancy name for them...like Gloria Valday or something...I didn't want something like Suzy Swartz...it had to sound like an actress. I'd say, 'Now ladies and gentlemen, for the girls in the audience tonight we have my handsome right-hand man and

Newspaper advertisement for Doctor Jekyl's Weird Show.
[Sanford Herald]

stage manager...Mr. Lynnnnnn Strange!!'...and then style him so he could come out and take a bow. He always got applause. The guys would boo, and the girls would giggle and applaud. Then I'd say, 'For the bachelors in the audience I've got the loveliest little actress you've ever seen. You've seen her on G. E. Theater on TV.' Well...she'd never heard of G. E. Theater but they didn't know it. Of course those guys would stomp and whistle. I mean she could be a plain girl...but as long as she had on next to nothing, they'd stomp, whistle, holler and carry-on...she'd get applause every time.

"In late '63 I take the ghost show out just for a few weeks. I thought it was going to be a few weeks but then I wound-up doing eight weeks of dates in the Southeast for Phillip Morris and his Stars Incorporated out of Charlotte, North Carolina. We were in Alabama, several spots in Georgia, Bob Cannon theaters, and all. Phillip Morris was a big timer who came on the scene in the mid-fifties and used the stage name of Doctor Evil. His shows were fast-paced and usually followed the Silkini format which had become a standard of most spook shows.

"Now in November 1963, we actually emptied the house with the ghost show when I played the Rose Theater in Meridian, Mississippi, which, at that time was the black theater. When the monster hit the stage and we went to the blackout, the house emptied. When the lights came back on there wasn't one face looking at me, the place was vacant...the whole place was empty! They had carried the damn popcorn machine out into the street. It was outside on the sidewalk next to the curb...the momentum of the people leaving the theater carried the popcorn machine out the front door. The manager was standing there shaking his head saying, 'Look at my popcorn machine.' That's the first house I officially emptied with my own ghost show, although, I emptied six or seven more later on.

"I was in Virginia when Karsten Enterprises called me from Redondo Beach, California, and said, 'Johnny Cates has fallen through a stage and broke his leg in thirty-two places, we need you to pick-up Johnny's route out here in California.'

"I left Staunton, Virginia, with the ghost show in December, 1963, after playing two months of dates for Stars Incorporated and dead-headed to San Leandro, California. I stopped off and spent a day in Houston with Johnny at his home...he was in a cast, using crutches and a wheelchair. What happened was...he was doing a big carnival thing, this was not a theater stage, he was doing the girl to gorilla illusion for a producer out of Houston while waiting for Joe Karsten to get these dates setup for his ghost show tour. Right in the middle of this one fair he was playing, the stage collapsed with him breaking his left leg in thirty-two places. The Karsten Agency booked both of us, this is why he called me to take Johnny's route. Karsten was the only man in America who could block-book theaters. He had California United Theaters, Manos Theaters in Pennsylvania, Panther Theater Corporation, Shine Theater Corporation, Paramount-Gulf theaters...across the Southeast, Louisiana, Mississippi. Paramount-Gulf had the big captain house in New Orleans, the Sanger Theater...the showcase of the Southeast. I went in there with my own show four years after playing it with Johnny Cates.

"It was Johnny Cates' ungodly accident that was the reason I picked-up that nationwide route. I'm serious, that's how I got that tour...of course I knew the Johnny Cates' show having been on it. He was the one who taught me the business...all Phillip Morris could do with Stars Incorporated was book those old T. D. Kemp theaters.

"On Christmas Eve night, 1963, I opened for California United Theaters in San Leandro. I literally picked up the route that Johnny Cates was to open on in San Leandro. I can't even remember all the towns we played...Chico, Oakland, and then up into Oregon. McMinnville, Eugene, Pendleton, Bend, yeah, all those towns, played them all.

"The one town in Oregon that everybody warned me not to play...was that big lumberjack town, Coos Bay. Everybody said call the theater and cancel the date. I said I can't do that, if I do that the whole chain is going to cancel on me. They were saying, 'Oh those lumberjacks they'll take you apart...they'll tear up your show.' Honest to God...I got into Coos Bay, we had about sixteen hundred people in the theater, standing in the back and all down the aisles, and from the backstage announcement all through the show...there was laughing and applause...I never had one smart aleck during the show...nobody threw a firecracker on stage...or anything like that. It was one of the finest dates I've ever played, one of my best audiences and one of the most appreciative audiences. When the show was over, I let my buddy start packing up and I changed jackets and walked out into the lobby and all those big ol' lumberjacks, and their wives, just wanted to shake my hand and compliment me on how much they enjoyed the show.

Yet this was the one everybody had told me not to play. But you can't do that, no, no, if you're going to be a prima donna like that you're going to be out of the business pretty quick.

"Now this was still the Doctor Jekyl Weird Show, my favorite title of all times. It was my show, my equipment, my monsters, my footlights, my switch panel, it was my show on Johnny Cates' route. The only thing that wasn't mine was the microphone. Johnny loaned me his microphone. He had the prettiest slim-lined microphone and insisted I take it because it was better than my old flat model plus his had an off and on switch. I still have that microphone.

"I took the Weird Show all over California and Oregon and played some very big houses and all of them were sold out. Unfortunately, I had to give up the last part of the Oregon route because my mother became ill and I had to come back to Florida and try to straighten things out and help out, get care for her and all.

"Karsten got another magician to cover the rest of my dates out there in Oregon. Well, I was home about five weeks or so, and by now it's early '64, and Joe Karston told me not to worry about anything because I'd be able to open in February.

Show poster from the Dr. Jekyl Weird Show
[Wise Collection]

41.

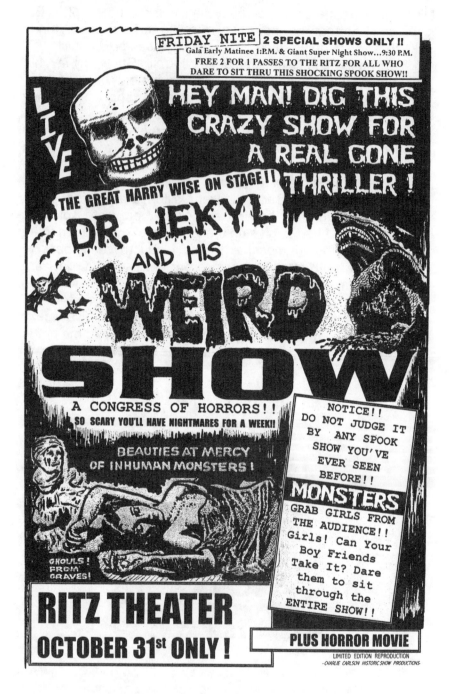

The last Weird Show poster ever printed was a limited souvenir item with a space provided in the upper left for Harry Wise's autograph.

Chapter 6

"We got two dollars and a meal in Atoka."

"In February 1964, I opened in eastern Pennsylvania, a tour that took us all up in the northeast, Ohio, New York, New England. We played all those theaters; Manos Theater Corporation, Panther theaters, Shine Theater Corporation. Now Shine was the biggest theater chain in America at that time and was based in Gloversville, New York.

"We even played the Ritz Theater on Staten Island. That was an experience because of getting on the ferry and going by the Statue of Liberty...it was the first time for a Florida boy like me, you can imagine that it was all very exciting.

"Then we played a theater up in Ogdensburg, New York, and got set up with about an hour to spare, so we got some chicken and went down to this park by the river. That was the St. Lawrence river that divides Canada from New York. Anyway, we're sittin' there having our chicken and a car came right across the park headed straight for the river...and it goes right out into the water. Lynn and I are sittin' there looking at each other...and watching this car making two or three circles out there in the river. Then it drives back out. It was the first amphibious car that we'd ever seen. It drives right past us and the guy waves at us. Me and Lynn are mystified, we'd never seen anything like that. After that, we see some people over at a little dock. We amble over there and of all things, there was a little girl that had been frolicking out there in the water and she had got out too far. It was all so stupid. She was only about five or six, and she gets out too far and is in trouble. She's hollering and shoutin'. Now there's seven people on that dock...they watch her go down...none of them can swim. I looked down at the edge of the dock and see that the water is only about four feet deep. I tell Lynn to hold my billfold and watch, and I sat down on the edge of the dock and just let myself down into the water. It was about chest deep on me...I walked out and got her in my arms and walked back up on the bank with her and laid her down. Somebody came up and started doing artificial resuscitation on her. Those people hailed me a hero, but I was just disgusted that nobody tried to wade out there and get her. It wasn't that deep, but it was a good thing we were there.

"We had another incident while going across Ohio when a semi-truck missed the bend and ran off the road and up the side of a small hill, or embankment. Lynn and I pull around it and stopped. We got up there to it and the driver was all slumped over the wheel. We helped the man out of his truck and got him over to the other side of the road. Another car had stopped and the driver knew where there was a farm house, about a half mile away. He went up there and called an ambulance and got him to the hospital. We thought he'd had a heart attack, but come to find out it was a coma, a diabetic coma, that had caused him to blackout. When I was a boy I wanted to be a hero...but I found out that being a hero can't be planned. You just have to be in the right place at the right time. You can't set it up, it just happens...it could happen anytime.

"In Fitchburg, Massachusetts, we did a Saturday morning matinee for the kids. I get a boy up from the audience for the guillotine act. He's down on his knees, locked in the guillotine, and I come down with the blade, and everything is fine. He looks up at me and I asked, 'Is everything fine, just nod yes.' That always got a laugh, but this time I couldn't get the blade back up. The damn blade got stuck down in the frame with the kid's head still in there. I couldn't get that blade back up. This was no bad gag, it was not part of the show, and here I am struggling trying to get the blade back up. The audience is laughing at me, and they're laughing at him. I finally told him, 'Stand up, take the legs of the guillotine in your hands, and hold the frame out straight.' So he stands up with his head still locked in the thing...and he is holding the guillotine horizontal to the floor. I help him off to the wings. It was the funniest-looking thing, by now I'm giggling to myself and the audience is dying with laughter. Now here's the payoff. I get him backstage and then got back on the microphone to try to get control of the audience. Meanwhile Lynn is back there with a hammer and chisel trying to take the guillotine apart and the mike was still on. Bang! Bang! Bang! You could hear him right over the mike. The audience was laughing, they were really losing it...and the manager was standing in back just convulsed in laughter. Lynn finally gives me the signal and walks out with the boy so everybody could see he was alright. The guillotine was laying in pieces back there in the wings. The manager actually asked me, 'Are you sure that's not part of the show? Don't you do that at every show?' I said, 'No sir, I do not...that's the only time that has ever happened.' It was about twelve minutes of mayhem unrehearsed, but they thought it was part of the act.

"We played the Bulldog Theater in Weatherford, Oklahoma, Mary Marten's hometown, that was in '64...it was a very small town. Lynn Ashe and I get into town...he really is the best man I ever had with me...but we get into town and see this little ol' theater. Lynn and I just look at each other and shake our heads. It was just a small town situation, a little theater, little stage, with curtains though, and a couple hundred seats or so.

"Well we get to the theater and start unloading and here comes the manager and he starts talking with us. I told him that we needed to fuse to thirty amps. He says, 'What? I can only fuse this place to twenty amps.' I said, 'Lord...you don't play many stage shows do you?' We had flash pots, amplifier, microphone, turntable, switch panel, light lines and everything. We needed thirty amps for the show, especially on the blackout with the flash pots and all. 'Well,' he said. 'I'll go talk with the man at the hardware store.' I said, 'What?' He said, 'Yeah, down the alley, I'll go in the back door and talk to him and maybe he'll let you plug into the hardware store.' So we took a hundred and twenty-five foot line...ran it out the back of the theater...down the alley and into the back of the hardware store. The man at the hardware store gave the theater manager the key to the hardware store so that when we were loading up at one in the morning, we could get in there and unplug the line. So...here's our electric coming out of the hardware store, down the alley and into the back of the theater to our switchbox.

"It gets time for the show, we turn-on the electric, and I make the backstage announcement and I make my entrance for the magic opening. It was only six minutes of magic,

45.

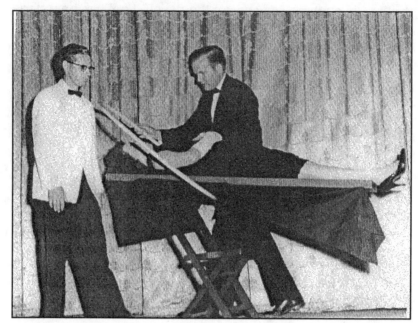

Lynn Ashe aka "Lynn Strange" on stage with Harry Wise.
[*Wise Collection*]

a couple of silk scarves, doves, and all that. But right in the middle of my beautiful magical opening the theater manager comes walking down the center aisle of the theater, right down to the footlights, and looks up at me and says, 'Doctor Jekyl...what did you do? The whole town just went dim!' When we had turned on the footlights, sound, and everything else for the opening we caused the town to go dim. Lynn was back there in the wings just laughing. We got through the show alright and got our line out of the back of that hardware store and packed-up. Now that actually happened, at the Bulldog Theater in Weatherford, Oklahoma. We dimmed the lights in the entire town.

"A couple of days later we pulled into Seminole, Oklahoma, and stopped in front of the theater. I got out to look at the marquee. I always liked to stand in front of a theater and marvel at my own Doctor Jekyl publicity campaign. I'm standing there on the sidewalk and up walks this big Indian girl, oh, about 300 pounds. She was about seventeen and had her little brother with her, I guess he was about nine years old. She overhears Lynn and I talking about the show and asks, 'Are you the mad doctor in the show?' I replied, 'I most

46.

certainly am, I'm Doctor Jekyl, how are you?' Then she asked me if I did magic tricks in the show. Well, I had a silver half-dollar in my pocket so I took it out and tossed it in the air and did the pretend catch, then I reached down and got it out from behind my knee. I did the French drop...and all...I was in fine form in front of that theater. Lynn is watching me doing tricks for that big Indian girl when all of a sudden she says, 'Why don't you give my little brother that half-dollar?' I said, 'WHAT? I ain't giving nobody my money...what's the matter with you?' She grabbed my right arm and jerked it up behind my back and brought me to my knees right there on the sidewalk! Well, there I was with this big 300 pound hulk of a girl looking down at me. She grabs the half-dollar out of my hand and takes off with her little brother down the sidewalk. I looked up and yelled, 'Lynn, what the hell happened?' I'm serious! Lynn is dying laughing at all this and just says, 'Harry just let those kids have that silly half-dollar.' That was the one time he wasn't my buddy, he didn't even chase after them. My arm was hurting and all he was doing was laughing, saying, 'That beat anything I ever seen. Did she break your arm? Do you reckon you'll be able to do the show tonight?' That's how I lost a half-dollar in Seminole, Oklahoma, right in front of the theater that I was going to play that night.

"We were driving all night going from Tulsa to somewhere and on the map it showed that we could cut across to the left on a new road. We took that road and drove about twenty miles and it just ended...right off into the sand. It just ended...there was nothing but sand, skunks, and cactus. Well we're cussing, but we get back up on the road and drive back to the main highway...the Will Rogers Parkway, it was rough as a cob, just like a washboard in those days. We stopped at a truck stop and went in for coffee. There was a truck driver sitting In there and the waitress was waiting on him, and we tell them about going forty miles out of our way. The waitress busts out laughing, 'That's our governor's work, that's a pork barrel project that won't never be finished.' Well, talk about a road to nowhere, we were on it in Oklahoma.

"Atoka, Oklahoma, now that's another story. As we were driving into Atoka, we noticed that all the businesses had liquidation sales going on. Some had already gone out of business. It looked like the whole town was going out of business. Lynn and I rode around the little town wondering why are we booked here? Anyway, we get over to the theater and there's an elderly man and his wife, they had owned the theater forty-six years or something. Very nice people but I've forgotten their names. The man says to me, 'Mister Wise, instead of running six newspaper mats, forty radio spots...I only ran six radio spots and one ad in the newspaper.' I said, 'What?' And he says, 'Our town's out of business, they're building the expressway out there and the town is shutting down. We'll be lucky if we get sixty or seventy people tonight.' I said, 'Oh lord, well since we're here we'll get set up and do you some kind of ghost show.'

"This was a wonderful man and his wife, and they lived under the stage in the basement, I guess they'd always lived there. But listen to this now. We go ahead and do the show...there's about seventy-four people or so, and we get all done and start packing up and the man comes backstage. He says to me, 'Mister Wise...after the radio spots, and the posters that came off the top, and the other expenses, you and I got four dollars to split. You'll get two and I'll get two. You're the last stage show we're going to play here...we're closing our doors next week...we're going out of business. Now would you please come eat something with us, my wife has mashed potatoes, green beans and roast beef, so come eat with us. So, we went downstairs and ate a nice meal that the man's wife had prepared. We got two dollars and a meal in Atoka, Oklahoma, but I won't never forget that, they were wonderful people. But it's symbolic of what has happened across this country to America's small towns and theaters and it's still going on today. Now big corporations run everything.

"There was another show we did in Oklahoma, it was a Sunday show which was an odd booking as we seldom played Sundays. I can't recall the name of the town, but we get there and get unloaded and the manager was nice. I did the guillotine routine where we supposedly chop a boy's head off. I asked for a volunteer from the audience and kids would raise their hands. I would usually point at one, or go down into the audience and kibitz a little then choose one. Once I had picked one, I'd be cueing him on what to do while walking up to the stage with him. Now this time I had picked a fat kid, he had on a red shirt, jeans, and a baseball cap. He looked exactly like Spanky McFarland of the Little Rascals. So I get back to the mike and I tell him, 'I'm going to call you Spanky, you look just like Spanky McFarland in the movies.' The audience laughed and he said, 'That's alright everybody here knows me, my name's John.' I said, 'Well John, I have something interesting to show you.' Then I took the cloth cover off the guillotine. He looked at it and stepped back. I said, 'John, this is the illusion I want you to help me with.' I brought the guillotine forward, took the top off it and told him to get down on his knees and to put his head in it. He gets down there with his head in the thing and I put the top back on. So he's now locked in the guillotine. He took his cues fine, it was funny and everybody was having a ball...and here's what happened. I had a skull that was in a basket under the guillotine. I picked the skull up and said, 'John, I want you to meet Charlie. He's been with us now several months and he's the only accident that we've ever had. His head came off in a show in Jacksonville, Florida.' Well, that boy looked at the skull, then back up at me...and he took off his baseball cap and started fanning himself and he said, 'Oh my lord, what have I gotten myself into.' The audience lost it. I stood there helpless, convulsed in laughter. He just took the show...fanning himself with his baseball cap. The audience loved it...you can't rehearse something like that, you can't cue something like that, it just has to happen.

"We got down to Sheffield, Alabama...there's a triangle of towns in that area, Sheffield, Muscle Shoals and another town...we played them all. In Sheffield we had a good house and did a nice show. There was this sixteen year old theater usher that was so impressed with the show that he followed us around and kept talking to us. Well, we're in the alley behind the theater loading the station wagon and getting ready to leave. I decided to drive to the next town so Lynn was sitting on the passenger side with the window rolled down. This boy, the usher, comes running out to see us off, saying, 'Oh you guys were wonderful, I really enjoyed the show.' Now Lynn was a smart aleck, we used to do all kinds of bits together that you wouldn't believe. Well, we're sitting there in the car with the motor running, and this kid, still overly impressed with the show, leans in the passenger side window and looks at Lynn and says, 'But...them ghosts...them ghosts you guys had in that big blackout...them ain't real ghosts are they?' Lynn looks at me, then he looks at the boy, then back at me...and he turns to the boy and screams right in his face! Just screamed as loud as he could sending that boy ricocheting backwards. At that same moment, I gunned it and we took off out of town in a cloud of dust. I haven't been back to that town since. That poor boy's ears are probably still ringing from that scream.

"So, I do all that with the Doctor Jekyl show, and I get back home...and Joe Karsten calls me and says that he had booked Florida State Theaters for October and November 1964 and wanted me to play it. But he said they wanted me to do a showcase date. I said, 'What, after me doing this thing all over America...you mean to tell me that Florida State Theaters wants me to do a showcase date?' He says, 'Yeah, they are sending some executives down to the Ritz Theater in Sanford since it's only about six blocks from your house...you're going to have to go over and do a show mostly for those executives.'

"That made me mad. If they couldn't look at my resume and all those grosses...State Theaters in Schenectady, New York, two-thousand people...Coos Bay, Oregon, sixteen-hundred. If they couldn't see that we were doing business...if they couldn't see that I could do it on stage...well that made me mad. Joe Karsten calmed me down and on October 16, 1964, I played my hometown theater, a morning show for the kiddie matinee and a night show at nine for the adults supposedly, which were a lot of teenagers. Well...the executives, in their suits and ties, came in and stood around the back of the theater. Bill Lovelace was the manager then, and after that morning show Bill came backstage and said to me, 'Harry after this morning's show, don't worry, you've got it. They already told me you've got the rest of the chain.'

"My mother came down to see that show and she could not believe the kids lined up at the theater, all the way down Magnolia avenue around the block to Palmetto avenue...two blocks of kids lined up. I built the promotion front on the Ritz to publicize that show, it stretched all across the front. Two weeks before this show, I had put Doctor Jekyl's oddity collection in the lobby. It was a big case, with all kinds of odd things I had collected. This was all publicity for the show. The Sanford Herald ran a story about how TV's Mr. Magic had turned himself into the dread Doctor Jekyl. It was a beautiful job, and that story appeared right next to the advertisement for the show in the paper.

"So here I am, in and out of town, I'm doing the entire Florida State Theater chain Friday and Saturday nights and still on the Uncle Walt show once or twice a week, usually Wednesdays and Thursdays. I'm Doctor Jekyl on the weekends and Mr. Magic on television during the week.

"On December 20th or 21st, after finishing the television show in Orlando, I left the studio and went downtown to meet my buddy Art Burris at Stroud's Drugstore on Church Street. I go in and he's eating a sandwich and having his coffee, and here's this blond waitress waitin' on him. So, I take a look at her and can't take my eyes off her beautiful, long, silk-like, blond hair. We're there an hour or better, talking and visiting, but I'm not paying any attention to Art...I can't take my eyes off that waitress. I'm asking her questions and all. Art finally says to me, 'Harry...please...can we have a conversation?' I told him I liked the girl and I started asking him about her but he got more disgusted with me. We're there about forty-five minutes...and when she brings us a coffee refill I asked her out. Well...she looked at me and said, 'No,' and turned-around and walked off. Well that was too much. I'm still looking at her and Art really gets disgusted...and he does this, he just slaps his hand on the counter and says, 'Sandy come here!' Well, she just looked at him and he says again, 'Come here Sandy, talk to me.' She walks over and looks at him across the counter and Art says, 'Sandy this really is Harry Wise, Mr. Magic, he really is on TV, and he does have his shows in Florida State theaters on the weekends...I know his parents, I often have Sunday dinner with them, he's telling the truth so let the guy take you out, let him take you to dinner.' Well, she looked at him and said, 'Oh, alright Art,' and turned and walked away. It was Art Burris that got me that date.

"Now talk about total and absolute vindication, here's the climax to this story. Art goes home, now she gets off at nine-thirty so I hung around and took her home in my car. We get to her house and go into the living room and here's her two brothers and three sisters, mother and dad, all sitting there watching TV. Her middle sister, Pam, jumps up and goes, 'Ahhhgg it's...Mr. Magic!!' Of course, that was wonderful and was total vindication right across home plate for me. Then the other kids jump up and they're coming over to talk and shake hands and all that. Her mother and father are just looking on and Sandy is looking at me. Well, we all had coffee and kinda got to know one another and Sandy and I made it up to go out the next night. On our first date we went to the drive-in to see 'Godzilla,' our first movie together was a horror movie!

"Now Sandy had never seen my show, never seen me on TV, but in February '65, I put her in my show. I even used her sister, Vickie, for a few dates with us, she was my floating lady on TV in Orlando. After dating Sandy for about four months or so, we got married and by March she was on the road with me.

51.

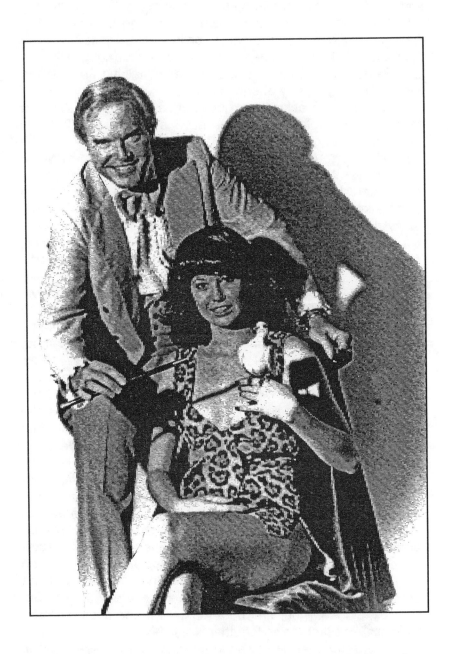

In the mid-1970s, Harry Wise, with his assistant Diana, carried his magic into nightclubs in an act called "Exotica." [Wise collection]

Chapter 7

"A Symphony of Magic and other Capers"

"We started segueing in '65 and '66 from the ghost show into a full magic show with phone promotions. By 1967 we were mostly doing a full two hour magic show with sponsors and advanced telephone solicitation. We featured big, flashy illusion acts...like the floating girl...scarves through the girl...those sort of things. Nobody seems to understand about that, when you go in to do a big auditorium show, with four people, illusions, comedy and all, you can't just go in there and hope the sponsor sells three or four tickets. You've got to put in an advance telephone promotion, sell tickets by calling people. You're three or four weeks in each town ahead of the show, we had to gross fifteen or twenty thousand to make it.

"One of the biggest phone promotions on our own that we did was in '66 in Griffin, Georgia for a VFW post. We were there five weeks staying in the old Griffin Hotel while doing the phone promotion. I called and had Johnny Valentine come up and be on that show. He was a good buddy and was an escape artist. Anyway, in Griffin there was a lady theater manager that worked for Martin Theaters and she ran the Griffin theater. Well, she wanted to book the ghost show so the second week we were in town I went and talked with her. So, she says, 'Look, leave me a film trailer and a couple of forty-by-sixties, a couple of posters and all, and I'll put them up. I know I can do it because I've been with the company several years and the main office will give me the okay.' I went ahead and left her the publicity material, which I always had in the car with me. Sure 'nuff, I went over to see her the next afternoon and she had already cleared it with her main office. I had to drive down to Florida to get the props for the show and we put the ghost show in her theater the night after the full evening show, 'Mr. Magic's Symphony of Magic,' at the high school auditorium. That was on Friday night. Then on Saturday night we did the ghost show at the Griffin Theater. We were the only shows in town.

"So here we were, in the Griffin Theater, ready to do the show and there's about 150 or 200 people in the theater, and I made the backstage announcement...'Here he is Doctor Jekyl' and all that...and make my entrance and a little boy in the second row with his mother says, 'Look mommy it's Mr. Magic!' I'll never forget that, and I bowed to them and greeted 'em...and said, 'Hey you guys saw the show last night didn't you?' He said, 'Yes sir, we enjoyed it.' After the ghost show, his mother and him hung around and we went out and talked to them. They had seen both shows. I had two ready-made fans right there in Griffin, Georgia.

"From 1963 to about '70, I gave Georgia a fit, I played just about every town in the state with my four units, Auction Dollar Days, the Doctor Jekyl Weird Show, the magic show with sponsors, and then for seventeen months in '69 and '70 I even ran a road show movie attraction called 'The Price of Sin.'

"Even though we were into the phone promotions and sponsored dates for the big magic show, we were still doing ghost shows whenever we could get a booking. Sandy had replaced Lynn on the ghost show, but Lynn would still come out with us on the phone promotions and the two hour show. Lynn Ashe eventually went out on his own for about seven years with a marionette show for Ross Southern Assemblies playing school assemblies. Ross could block-book schools, which cut independent guys like me out of the school business.

"Now the third or fourth show that Sandy did with me was at the beautiful Temple Theater in Meridian, Mississippi. I had played here before, back in 1963. We're ready to open and I get on the mike and make the opening announcement...'we're glad to see you' and all that...and I start asking for volunteers to come up on the stage. Well this beautiful young woman, about twenty-four or five, raises her hand. Now I normally picked teenage boys and girls, but anyway...I go down there and escort her up to the stage. That's when I smelled it on her...she was drunk. I didn't know she was drunk when I picked her...Sandy always said that I knew it...but I didn't. I should have never got her up there, but I did. She's saying things like, 'Oh Doctor Jekyl, you sure are good looking, you're the nicest man I ever met' and the mike is picking this stuff up and the audience is laughing. I didn't mind that...I mean we were all laughing. I get her to the stage and sat her down in the chair next to some other kids. Then I get the other kids up and do the hypnotic bits, where we tell one boy that a broom is a girl and he strokes the broom like he's making love to a girl and all that. Sometimes I'd use my coat instead of a broom, it always brought the house down. The whole time this drunk girl keeps making side remarks but she was funny. I did a floating skull routine, where I floated a skull down in front of the kids and over their heads. When it got to the drunk girl she said, 'Don't let that thing bite me!!'

"Well...now it was time for the guillotine, after which I planned to dismiss them from the stage to do the blackout. So, I get this little nine year old boy up and I do all the intro stuff about being brave, forthright, courageous, and all this. Then I go over and get the guillotine and pull the drape off of it. And he looks at it, looks at me...and looks back at the guillotine. I removed the top and told him to come around behind it and place his head in it. The audience is laughing...but I wasn't saying anything funny...but then I saw Sandy in the wing with her arm over her mouth going, 'Ohhhh!!' I look down...and there is an ever-growing puddle beneath the kid. That boy was peeing like a horse right there on stage! I knew he was nervous, but I never knew he was about to have a nervous breakdown. I'm not exaggerating...it was a puddle and the drunk girl said, 'Oh poor kid Doctor Jekyl, he's scared to death...look at him!' That only made the whole audience laugh harder...and me too. Of course the poor kid was embarrassed...he couldn't help it...it just scared the pee out of him. I said to him, 'Look, I can tell you're probably a little scared...so how 'bout you go on back down in the audience and enjoy the rest of the show and I'll get somebody else up here and we'll go on with it.' Sandy was mad at me for laughing, but between that boy and the drunk beautiful one, it brought the house down. I guess I left him traumatized for life, I don't know...but it was sure funny.

"The biggest menagerie that I ever had was four doves, one bunny rabbit, two guinea pigs, two ducks, and a chocolate-brown poodle dog named Pepi LeTail. I would do a thing with the poodle using a green scarf and another using a doggie bone, it was a sucker trick, but the kids loved it. Pepi had been with us for several years, a wonderful little dog. He was as popular with the kids as the rabbit was. I was up in North Florida playing a couple of dates and Sandy wasn't watching him and he got run over by a car one night. I lost the favorite dog of my life and part of my act that night.

"In December '68 I was on a big variety show in Jacksonville called the Startime Christmas Benefit with Johnny Weissmuller, star of the old Tarzan movies.

"For a brief period in 1972, I went into the side show business. Now I've never told people about this because it was the reigning flop of my entire career and it still resounds in my memory like an earthquake. I wanted to do something different so I put together a side show for carnival consumption. It was a five-and-one, not a ten-and-one where there are ten acts in one show. A layman might not understand those carnival terms, but I had a five-in-one. I took Norman White and billed him as *Big Milo Fontaine*. He weighed 510 pounds and we billed him as 600 pounds. We took an old boat trailer and converted it into a fold-out stage, then I had two eight and a half foot banners painted for the front. I bought canvas from an army surplus store and made my own tent. We built the whole show from the ground up. I booked it with two different carnivals, Cumberland Valley Shows and Gold Medal Shows to play fairs in Kentucky, Tennessee, and North Carolina.

"I had a good-looking front, two big banners with spot lights, one was the magician floating the lady and the other featured the world's largest magician Big Milo. I taught him a few tricks and he would do magic and answer questions about his size. We had the hype on him, like he could eat two loaves of toast for breakfast, a dozen eggs, and a pound of bacon. Which he could really do, he was no picky eater. I mean it cost something to feed him, lets not talk about moving money or privilege fees... or running out for a hamburger... Milo could eat. Originally he had worked for me as a phone man on promotions in Orlando, he could sell on the phone and the first day he brought in a couple of hundred dollars for us. But we did not do so well with the side show.

"I even had John Moss of Knoxville come over and talk for us. I had seen him work on carnivals, on the girl shows, he was the handsomest man, fully ward-robed and a true Southern gentleman. He always looked good on that bally platform and was one of the best bally talkers that was ever on any midway. I couldn't believe it when John came over to do my openings.

He suffered three or four weeks of that flop with us. This was in April and May and the weather was pretty bad, the lots were muddy, and that was part of the problem. I don't know, maybe we had the wrong act...my lead was a fat man. We were right next door to the Wrestling Bears...now if you want competition...everybody paid to see the Wrestling Bears. On the other side of me was the Girl Show...that's where John Moss should have been working. I was stuck in the middle of the money and couldn't get a nickel. One night we grossed eleven dollars and next door two hundred people were going in the girl show on a bad night! We died the death of a dog the first day out...I couldn't make a nickel with that show. We finally folded in Shelby, Tennessee, and I went back to doing something that I knew how to do.

"Now in 1971, to about '73, except for that brief side show folly, I played a few nightclubs as Darkvale. This was in addition to doing the big magic shows. As Darkvale I played the Pillow Talk Lounge in Cocoa, clubs in Jacksonville, and Joey Stanwood's Diamond Show Lounge in Orlando. It had been a Go Go joint, but Joey turned it into a bar and supper club. He built a stage in there so he could do his Sinatra act. His wife, Nicki Loring, was a belly dancer, these were wonderful people. Joey had been a big timer up North in the nightclubs. He did his Sinatra songs and would emcee everything, and I would come out as Darkvale for the magic.

"Darkvale came about...well I stumbled across the name in 1969...but never printed it on a poster until later. I only did one or two full evening shows under this name. I mainly held the Darkvale act to the clubs, usually Friday or Saturday nights because we were doing phone promotions during the days for the full evening shows. I billed the act as Ray Darkvale...but you'll see it spelled two different ways. I never could make-up my mind If I wanted to spell it 'Dark-v-a-l-e' or 'Dark-v-e-i-l.' Really, it should be 'v-a-l-e,' like a dark place in the valley. A misprint in some of my business cards even spelled it 'Dardveil.' But all this was in addition to my full evening show.

"I was passing through Kissimmee, Florida one day, in 1973, and saw a circus set up in a lot. I stopped and went over to visit it. I got to talking with the owner, Wayne Franzen, and asked him if I could hang around and announce the show. Now I was just in regular clothes, but he let me announce the acts and thought that I did a remarkable job. That was the Franzen Brothers circus. I later became the ringmaster for this show.

"Even after I started doing the full evening show, I still booked my ghost show with a few independent theaters just to get it out of my system. Now, the last midnight ghost show tour I did was in '73. Guy Trump was with me on that one. We did a week in Texas, opening in Kermit, then did a week in Arkansas playing Fort Smith, Pine Bluff, Eldorado...towns like that. Then we dead-headed up to Detroit and crossed into Canada to open in Windsor, Ontario. Guy was only a teenager, but he became my driver, electrician, and played the monster that grabbed the girls out of the audience. We tried to fulfill our promotion that said 'monsters grabbed girls from the audience.' That we could do. Now as for the statement that said we could 'bring the dead back to life'...well...we never really fulfilled that part of the promotion.

"Guy was wonderful, he knew the whole show, the flash pots, sound, electrical, and all. He later became the electrician with the Sells and Gray Circus. Canada was the last tour for my midnight ghost show, but the last actual Doctor Jekyl Weird shows, were in New Smyrna Beach, Florida, and in an independent house in Daytona, that was about 1974 or '75. Johnny Valentine, the great *Prince of Escape* played with us on those dates. Johnny was a first class escape artist. After doing those dates, the ghost show ended. It was the last real ghost show on stage in America. After Sandy and I divorced in '74, I went on with the two hour show.

"On the big two hour magic show we used three titles, *The Symphony of Magic*, *Wonder Show of Curioddities* and *Mr. Magic's Top Hat Capers.* I've always been into titles and logos. The reason for using various titles has to do with promotion. We didn't want to use the same title again in the same area. We might do a show for a sponsor, then eight months later book another show in the same area...you can't use the same title. Now I had enough stuff to change the show and keep it fresh...but the title had to be changed too or people would think they were seeing the same show. For instance, we played some volunteer fire department promotions eight or nine years in a row. I played my own hometown Civic Center in Sanford once or twice every year for various sponsors like the Elks, the Optimists, Kiwanis, and other civic organizations.

"In 1968, as a publicity stunt for a show sponsored by the Elks Lodge, I even drove an automobile while blindfolded right down through town which got some good press.

"In '76, and '77, in addition to my big show, I did a nightclub magic act called 'Exotica.' My assistant on this one was a former dancer, showgirl…and a true goddess, named Diana.

"The sponsors of my big two hour show did some really good things raising funds for needy causes. I was the Goodwill Ambassador for the Florida Elks for four years, from 1968 through 1972. I raised enough money to get twenty-two kids operations at the Harry-Anna Crippled Children's Home. We would go over there each Christmas and each Easter and do a special show just for those kids.

"For the Forest City, Florida, Volunteer Fire Department we were the first fund raiser they ever had and we got them their first tanker truck. Down in Brevard county, Florida, I helped raise enough funds to save a home for wayward girls…the Hacienda Girls' Ranch that was in financial trouble.

"In 1977, at the Spring Lakes Volunteer Fire Department in Orange City, Florida, we put on our big promotion and show and got their first *Jaws-of-Life*. We did a six week promotion and show. They wanted a Jaws-of-Life so they went ahead and ordered it and it came in while we were still there. Now this is a strange story because I was there to see it used for the first time. We had done the show, but we had to go in and take care of the last pieces of mail and settle the last few bucks with the committee. We're sitting there taking care of business in the fire department a couple days after the show and we hear an ungodly noise out on the highway. The fire department was right on highway 17-92. When we heard all this noise I got up and went over to the window and said, 'There's a bad car wreck right out there, I'm looking at it!' So the fellow I was working with was one of the firemen and he said, 'My god that's our jurisdiction, I better call it in.' So he dials the fire department's emergency number, which is just through the door, in the next room, about twenty feet from where we were. Well, about eight guys come running in and get the emergency ambulance and go out the door and up to the corner, a half a block or so. When they got there they found the man trapped in his car and they used that Jaws-of-Life to get that man out of that wreck. He had a crushed ankle. That was the first time they used that new Jaws of Life and I was there to see it.

"In 1978 I met my second wife, Denise, in Orlando. I was forty-three and she was twenty-two. I took her to dinner at a restaurant, out by the airport although we had only met a couple hours earlier. She was beautiful, a dancer and a model, and had been a majorette in her hometown of Butler, Pennsylvania. It was like a movie script, Denise asked me all the right questions like, 'Do you use a real magic wand in your act?' She asked if I had a top hat and a cape, and if I used a real rabbit like seen on television. Of course I answered yes but she was being sincere. We had to wait forty-five minutes after ordering dinner so we had this whole long preamble before dinner. She said that she had never seen a real magician in her life except for a couple on TV. I said, 'What? You've never seen a real magician?' Well...we had an enjoyable evening and I took her home but couldn't get her out of my mind.

"The next day I wrote her a couple page letter...on my letterhead so she'd know I meant business. I drove over to her place but she wasn't home. I always carry some scotch-tape in my car for whatever, so I taped the letter to her door. I hung around and ate dinner, went to a couple of clubs, but didn't run into her anywhere so I got back home about one o'clock in the morning and went to sleep.

"About eleven o'clock the next morning the phone rings. It was her on the phone. She said, 'Did you mean what you said in that letter?' And I said, 'Well, yes, that's why I put it on my letterhead so you'd know I meant business.' Then she said, 'Maybe you'd better come get me, I'm going to start packing.' Well, what can you do and what can you say? I got her a bouquet of roses and headed over to Orlando and picked her up and she moved in with me. A couple of weeks later she was part of the show. We'd rehearse right there on the front porch of the house on Sixth Street. She was great because she'd get it in one rehearsal and if she didn't she'd always ask to go over it again.

"I taught her a tandem act, where we'd work together on a twelve minute sequence. I would produce the silk scarves and toss them to her and she'd change the colors. Or I would tie them together and toss them to her and she would make a magic pass over them and separate them, things like that. She was a wonderful assistant and even other magicians loved it, they said they had never seen anybody work like that with their assistant. But, I really created a monster with her because the kids loved her. I was always used to stepping out and signing autographs and talking with the kids...now they wanted to talk with *Miss Magic*. She'd have to come out after each show and talk and sign autographs with everybody.

60.

"On August 26, 1978, we got married at the courthouse in Atlanta, Georgia. We went to seven different judges to marry us but were told by a secretary in the courthouse that judges don't do that anymore and said to try the prison minister from the county prison. Well, we had a couple of dates booked so we had to get the blood tests and get married and everything, but I was saying to myself, 'A prison minister?' It just didn't sound right to me but we went ahead and set it up. Now that was the only out-of-body experience I ever had....we were there in that courthouse getting married and the man was saying the words and all...and I look up at this fan rotating above us and it was like I was up there looking down on the ceremony. In my mind I was saying, 'Harry this is all wrong.' I knew not to get married at forty-three to a beautiful, twenty-two year old woman...but I did...and we had two good years together and did many great shows together.

"We carried the big magic show all over Georgia, Florida, Mississippi, Kentucky, and Tennessee. A promoter might call from anywhere asking for us to come up and do a show. We could get five hundred dollars for a show back then and they'd cover our gas and motel for one or two nights. Bob Craig, a promoter in Tennessee, would put us up in a first class room at the Holiday Inn and would always put us on the marquee out front...'Mr. Magic and Company is staying with us.' It'd make us feel so good. I mean here we were on the damn motel marquee! Bob Craig was a good promoter and would always come back to the room with us and count out the cash for us...five hundred or seven-fifty for the day depending on how far we had to drive. I knew he was grossing ten or twelve or fifteen thousand dollars and I would always say something like, 'Now come on Bob, we need more gas here, we're going to get breakfast before we get out of this town...we need to eat'...and he'd always toss me another fifty or seventy-five.

"In November 1979, I was featured as the special guest star on the big Holiday Magicland show in Lake City, Florida.

"I don't know where you could do phone promotions for a sponsor anymore. The state started shutting down the promoters and volunteer fire departments were the first to phase out. Now many of these same sponsors simply beg for handouts at intersections...you get no show...no carnivals, not even a bake sale because somebody might get sick and sue the sponsor. It has ruined show business and fund raising...all because of the government and a litigation crazy society.

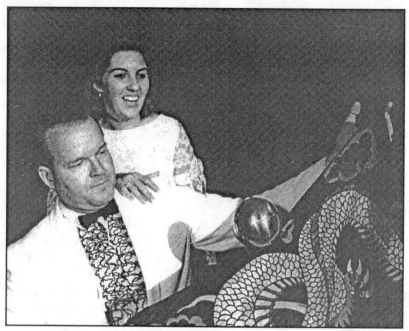

Magician Harry Wise doing the floating ball routine.
[Wise collection]

"I went into Savannah, Georgia, in 1984, or '85, and booked the Civil Air Patrol to sponsor a show...I mean I had it signed on a contract! Forty-eight hours later, I get back home and the guy calls me and says, 'Mr. Wise, I'm sorry but we can't do this...the Atlanta office just passed a rule...we can't ever have a carnival or show again.'

"I saw my whole world start disintegrating, full evening shows, magic shows, phone promotions...all gone. There was a time when I could go into a town and rent the local armory for fifty bucks, with another twenty-five for clean-up or else we did the clean-up ourselves. But you can't do these promotions anymore. It is one of the main reasons we shut down the big evening shows...plus the state wanted a hundred thousand dollar bond from every promoter. You had to put up your show, your rolling stock, your home or whatever you owned...and if you got into a little bit of trouble you'd lose everything.

"We were the fund raisers for these sponsors but it got to where if somebody complained...the sheriff would come out and yank the phones out. It didn't matter if you weren't doing anything wrong...all they needed was one complaint, or not even a complaint...it could just be a simple inquiry about where the money was going. In the end, everybody loses.

Chapter 8

"It's amazing at what you can get away with as a mentalist."
Hans Voglar

According to an old show card from a Jacksonville, Florida, nightclub, *Hans Voglar* was an "Internationally acclaimed hypnotist with thirty years experience." His "uncanny ability in the World of ESP had amazed audiences around the World" and he could read your thoughts. In showbiz that's promotion, but the truth is, Hans Voglar was really Harry Wise.

"I got into mentalism...all that was mostly in 1981, and it was a theraputic thing for me because I had just had a fiasco love affair that had lasted eight or nine months. I won't go into all that, but it left me devastated and by the time I got down to Florida I was a wreck. I spent two weeks in St. Augustine with my buddy Don Davison. He had been a ventriloquist, magician and film producer...and had written several books on mentalist acts. He said, 'Look, I can get a booking or two for a mentalist.' He gave me a couple of books on mentalism and I already had some material, so I started some late night reading and making notes. I'd never done a mentalist act. It became theraputic in the sense that I got into it instead of the bottle.

"It took me a couple of months to get it together. The first thing that I got myself was a set of ESP cards. Doctor J. B. Rhine created ESP cards years ago at Duke University for ESP experiments. I got to reading about mentalism, and the truth is...there are three or four principals of magic involved in a mentalist routine. So right up front I had several things that I could adapt to my mentalist act.

"I created three or four things like a prediction thing, and used a deck of playing cards called the Svengali deck.

63.

The World's Most Amazing Attraction

WILL HE
READ YOUR MIND?

In Person!

V O G L A R

THE MAN WITH THE XEROX MIND

Presents...

"MIRACLES of the MIND"

"As the radio transmits the voice, and the television transmits the picture...surely doth the mind transmit the thought!"

Above: An advertisement promoting the amazing Hans Voglar's 1981 appearance and mentalist act in Palatka, Florida.

My friend Burling Hull invented the Svengali deck in 1911 as *Cards Mysterious*...and I've seen his patent for those cards right there at his house. Years later, a magician from Chicago was selling them on TV as 'TV Magic Cards,' just about every magician has used the Svengali deck.

"For the most part, mentalism is psychology...you learn about reading people, their body language, mannerisms, their dress, and you can do a cold reading of some people and they'll think that you're some kind of a miracle worker. I found out that I had been doing a lot of this stuff in magic...in many cases I just repackaged magic as mentalism. I had to get a blackboard and chalk because there's times when you're reading a person's thoughts in the act and have to write it, or whatever, on the blackboard. It's all part of the act for the audience. I laid out some flyers and newspaper ads for the act and Don booked me in the Holiday Inns in Palatka and Jacksonville, one over in Pensacola, and I booked a show with the Seminole Community College. I played several night clubs, three or four colleges, a club in Winter Park, and the Diamond Show Lounge in Orlando.

"I used the name Hans Voglar. The name came from my mother's maiden name, she was Helen Margaret Voglar. I told her that someday I was going to use Voglar somehow...and sure enough it came about in 1981 with me as Hans Vogler the mentalist. My Voglar business card had on it 'ESP,' and under that was, 'Extra Sensitive Personality.'

"It's amazing what you can get away with as a mentalist. I mean it's much more blatant than being a magician. The truth is...mentalism is a very subtle kind of trickery. Now I never used electronic devices where some assistant in the wing is cueing me...and I never used the thing where the audience fills out a card when they come into the auditorium...like prayer cards used by some so-called religious healers to get information on people. I would not get into any of that because then you're getting into such blatant chicanery. I would come out clean with one brief case and do an hour to an hour and twenty minutes of good entertainment.

"I did a lot of interplay with the audience...but what got heavy for me...was answering a bunch of questions after the presentation. In the colleges, and night clubs too, but especially the colleges, these young people...college students...would come up to me and want me to be their guide. Can you believe it? They actually thought I was some kind of psychic! That's one reason why I eventually got out of the mentalist business. It was almost scary, they wanted somebody to predict the future for them. I don't quite know how to explain it...now I can understand being in a theater with the monster on stage, and waving a luminous piece of cheese cloth like it was a ghost and scaring some kids. I can understand that...that was Doctor Jekyl. But with the mentalist audience...everything was so refined, sophisticated, and everything...these were educated people...college people, they'd believe it was real...I'm talking about supposedly educated people...I could not believe how gullible they were. These were future lawyers, business people...political leaders...teachers...and all. That was what was so scary.

"Young adults...they'd always corner me after the show, they'd line up ten or fifteen people at the colleges...all wanting positive input. I could have held those people in the palm of my hand, I'm serious. They were so gullible, and so uncertain, I couldn't believe it. So many young women that were so insecure...and the young men were just as bad. I had one young girl at the college say to me, 'Mr. Voglar, my parents have always told me I couldn't be a designer, tell me what to do." I said, 'Of course you can be whatever you want. Take art, meet people that are designers and talk to them...and just go out here in the world and do it. There'll be a job for you somewhere.' God, you should have seen her beam. I could have told her all that without being Voglar. I could have been a guy off the street saying the same thing but she would not have listened. But with me dressed up as the Amazing Voglar in that blue suit and tails, she listened to anything I had to say.

"Now Hans Vogler was me...Harry Wise from Sanford, Florida. See what I mean...it's all such a facade, such an act, and it just shows that all anybody knows is what they think they see. Politicians do this all the time and get out there and lie and people believe them. But Vogler didn't go out there to mesmerize or exploit...he was there just to entertain and make a buck. I never professed to be from a university or anything like that. I did a couple of things with the ESP cards and would mention that they were created by J. B. Rhine of Duke University and all like that...it was all part of the patter. But I didn't have anything to do with any university...I already told you that I dropped out of the ninth grade...and here I was leading around college students...and even the faculty.

"One time I was doing a thing I had done many times

before...that Don Davison had taught me...but this one time it didn't work. You see, magic shops sell stuff for mentalists too...and they had what was called a 'Crystal Tear.' It was a small crystal thing that you'd sit on a little pedestal on the table. There's a gimmick to it and after you set it up, it would explode after about twenty minutes. The test was to hold it in your hand and it would get warm as you told the people about the Crystal Tear. I'd tell the whole audience that I wanted them to concentrate with me on the Crystal Tear. I would then sit the thing on the pedestal so they could see it. Now when it works it is the most beautiful, mystical-looking thing in the world...it would explode and the audience would believe they caused it by concentrating on it. Well...this time I couldn't get that thing to explode...I would've had to take a brick to this damn thing to make it explode. After the third time of failing with it, I just told them...'ladies and gentlemen I'm very sorry, there's either something wrong with me or there's something wrong with every one of you.' It was a flop...but this one young man comes up to me after the show, grabs my hand and shook it, and says, 'Mr. Voglar, I was doubtful of you until that tear thing failed...that's what convinced me that you're real.' That was the last time I used the Crystal Tear thing in the act.

"I played this night club in Jacksonville and did this seven key thing. You pass out seven keys to the audience and then mentally locate the one key that unlocks a padlock. It's a good routine, well this one woman fell in love with Voglar after that act. She pursued me for three or four days. I finally had to tell her, 'Hey look there's nothing that can come of this.' But it showed me how lonely she was, how insecure she was, and how damn gullible she was. If she had known that I started out as a house painter ordering tricks from comic book ads....she would have said 'oh pooh on Voglar!' All of this incredible gullibility and stupidity...and insecurity...I couldn't believe that my fellow humans could be that way. It was a real lesson in human psychology.

"My opinion of ESP and telekinesis...well it falls short of being reality. Telekinesis is supposedly where you can use the mind to move an object...mind over matter...but that's been debunked by the Amazing Randi. James Randi, he was the magician and skeptic that exposed Uri Gellar's mental spoon bending and all that stuff. There could very well be something that we don't know about but everything that I ever did with magic or mentalism, was brought about by natural means.

67.

"I know that some things can't be explained. One time, me and my friend was in a St. Augustine bookstore looking for a book called "100 Horror Stories," and they didn't have any left. They thought they had sold the last copy. A couple of nights later we go back in there and were walking down through the aisle of books and this book goes bloop...and falls out of the shelve on the floor, right at our feet. I reached down and picked it up...it was '100 Horror Stories!!' We just stood there looking at it. Now is that a coincidence? It would be a miracle million to one chance of that ever happening...but it happed to us. Now there was no reason for this to happen, there were no ghost in there pushing it out...I don't think there was any poltergeist involvement or anything like that. I can't believe in it yet it happened to us. I never had that happen again.

"Voglar, in a lot of ways, was fun. It was a different approach but I found out one thing, I liked the magic show better. As Voglar, for the most part, I had to act serious...but as Mr. Magic and Wise the Wizard, the largest part of the show was cutting the fool with the audience and making them laugh. I'll be honest...I had to back away with Voglar.

"I only did it for about a year and a half. In fact everything is so scattered now that if you wanted me to do an hour as Voglar I would have to search to find my notes and stuff that I used to have just to do it. I don't even know where my black board is. The last show I did as Voglar was on May 1, 1982, at a club in Jacksonville, Florida. As a mentalist you don't get to kibitz with the audience like a magician does. I liked it, but mentalism was not as much fun as being a magician.

Chapter 9

"I ran away with the circus at forty-six"
Harry Wise

"It's true that I ran away with the circus at forty-six years old. In 1982, my path crossed again with the Franzen Brothers circus when it was set up in St. Augustine, Florida. I went over to the lot to visit the owner, Wayne Franzen, and got to talking with him. He said, 'Oh, remember you well. I like your act and your voice." He had remembered me from Kissimmee back in '73 when he let me announce his show...and later, in 1975, Wayne had seen me do a big show at a KOA campground when I was barnstorming a couple of campgrounds. So we went across from where he was set up and had dinner and I ended up signing a deal right there to go with the circus.

"The Franzen show was a European style circus, meaning it had one ring. I loved the one ring because everybody was a star. The audience didn't have to watch three rings...all the attention is focused on that one ring.

"I went on the circus as a star. I did not go on there as a roustabout...I never had to lay my hands on canvas. I was the ringmaster for the show billed as *Wise the Wizard, Florida Television's Original Mr. Magic.* I love the word 'ringmaster,' although some call it a circus announcer. Under the canvas, the ringmaster is the manager of the show. He lays out the acts, and talks with the acts. He's got to pace the acts, like the ground acts or aerial acts. You can't have animals out there leaving crap for the ground acts to walk in or slip up in.

"I also did a featured magic act in the ring...I had my notes already prepared from years before just in case I ever went out with a circus. I had figured out acts that could be performed with a surrounding audience. In a theater the audience is in front, but in a circus they are all around you. So when I went with Franzen, not only did I have it all down on paper, I had the props and the wardrobe, cape and top hat and all. I even had a fine automobile, an Oldsmobile Vista Cruiser, and my trailer and all. Oh, I was ready for anything in those days.

"Wayne had a cat act, he was an animal trainer just like Clyde Beatty was...a tiger and lion act. That was what I'd talk about going around town on the sound truck...I'd talk about 'America's favorite animal trainer, Wayne Franzen, and he's here in your town!' I'd sell it, I'd really get with it.

"I really get disgusted with people who don't know what a circus is. When I was on the front door of the Franzen circus, I could have shot many people for asking where the rides were. They are American and don't know a circus from a carnival.

"In 1982, in Monmouth, Illinois, we were on a muddy clay lot and I couldn't get my car to move out of that slippery mud. Wayne Franzen hooked Ohka up to the front bumper of my station wagon. I sat inside and steered while Ohka the elephant pulled me and that station wagon, and my trailer, out of that mud and across that lot and out to the highway.

"Circus life is demanding, a circus is constantly moving from one town to the next. The show pulls onto a vacant lot and magically turns it into a place of entertainment and fun. The first thing that is done is to stake out the lot for the big top, which is nothing more than a canvas theater. The big difference is that in the theater the audience sits in front of the stage and in the big top the audience surrounds the acts and the ring is the stage.

"There is a lot involved with moving a circus, there are animals to feed and transport, fuel for the trucks and the generator that furnishes all the show's electrical power, and there are permits, and other things that theaters never have to worry about. The circus is a self-contained community that works, lives and travels together and it has to stay on the move regardless of weather. The old saying "keep the show on the road" applies more to a circus than any other form of entertainment. By the time the crowd is leaving the last show at night, roustabouts have already started loading out, the top is dropped, the canvas rolled and poles loaded and within hours the lot is vacant again and the show is on its way to the next town. Most circuses use an advance man that is a day or more ahead of the show, depending on the size of the show. The advance man gets the advertising in order and often handles the required license, permits, or whatever the show will need when it arrives. Most jumps between towns are done in the middle of the night so as to be on the next lot in the morning. I would sometimes leave at night and other times I would catch-up with the show the next morning.

"I'd pull into town and would get my stuff ready and then I would play hooky for a couple of hours. I would ride around the towns looking for a second-hand book store, magazine stand, and would always look for a little independent downtown restaurant to get me a good meal. I would take care of anything that I needed to do, get my mailings done, maybe get a tire for the car, or get on a pay phone and call my mom to see how she was doing or whatever. Then I'd get back to the circus in time to get on the sound truck and go around and bally the town for an hour or two. I used to enjoy that because I'm a talker anyhow.

"It was another world, the applause, the laughter, when all those people around you are laughing, well, there's no life like it. I could never choose the life of being a non-entity. I loved it.

"I took leave from the Franzen show in late summer to visit some friends in Greencastle, Indiana, the Lunsfords of the Tommy Tyme circus. Their winter quarters was in Greencastle, the circus later worked out of Milledgeville, Georgia, but the Lunsford home place was still in Indiana. Tommy Lunsford was the son of Richard and Laura Lunsford. While I was there, we visited a most enchanted place of covered bridges, a mill, on the Racoon river near Mansfield. There's no other place like it, it was like déjà vu...like I had been there before.

"I also stopped by and visited Tex Terry while I was up there and spent an evening with him at his place. He lived up on a hill and drove a big Cadillac with big bullhorns on the hood. Tex had made two-hundred westerns and played in the old Gene Autrey and Lone Ranger movies. He played an outlaw, stage driver, and stuff like that...in movies and television westerns. Tex Terry owned a restaurant up there and on Saturdays he would stretch-up a sheet on the wall and show some of his old westerns. People came from all over to see them. He died a few years ago at 88, but once and awhile, I still see him in old movies.

"The last date I played with Wayne Franzen was several years later in 1991, down at the St. Lucie County Fair in Fort Pierce, Florida. I had already played there three times before with my own ghost show. The circus was on the backend of

Johnny's United Shows that had the midway. The Fair committee had paid the circus a flat fee to be there as a free attraction. The people just walked in and sat down and we did three or four shows a day down there. But that was the last time I played with the Franzen circus.

[Note: On May 7, 1997, while performing before an audience of two hundred school children in Carroltown, Pennsylvania, Wayne Franzen was attacked and killed by one of his Bengal tigers. Following this tragic incident, the management of the circus was taken over by his son].

"Well, one circus led to another and 1983, I went out with Bill Blizner's Circus Royal out of Brickton, New Jersey. It was a one ring show and I joined it as the ringmaster with a magic act. I left Sanford, Florida, and dead-headed to Howell, New Jersey, where the show was to open. But, I get in there a day early and the Beatty-Cole circus was playing twenty-six miles from Howell, so I unhooked my trailer and went over to visit friends that I knew from Deland, Florida, and saw the night show up there. The Clyde Beatty-Cole circus has their winter quarters in Deland, Florida.

"The next day we opened our tour in Howell. It was a six week tour. We did Howell, then dates in New York, Ohio, New Hampshire, Massachusetts...then we spent four days in Maine. We played Portland, Maine, at a big shopping center. Then we turned around and on the way back hit a couple of dates in New Hampshire and Ohio.

"I remember one time the elephant man, Buck, didn't show up because he had truck problems on the road. Anyway, we were setting-up behind a big school up there in Massachusetts, and don't ask me the name of the town because I can't remember it. The guys get the tent all laid out and everything all set, but no elephant to pull it up. It's getting late, it was already about four-thirty in the afternoon. Well, I'm in my trailer reading and Dave came and knocked on my door and says, 'Harry we need you.' To which I replied, 'No you don't.' And he says, 'Yes, we need your station wagon, we need this fine Vista Cruiser to bring the top up.' Anyway we get the car in place and he hooks the main guy rope to my trailer hitch on the car...and me and my Vista Cruiser became the elephant. Dave walked right along beside me and told me when to gun it or when to stop. Just like he did with the elephant. Me and my old Vista Cruiser brought that top up that afternoon. I couldn't believe it, I got out and looked at that Big Top and felt kinda proud for doing what elephants had been doing for years.

72.

"I had several friends on the show, the Chimp Lady as I called her, she had a chimpanzee act. There was Trina and Danny DuVal, they were about the top circus acts at the time. Every morning Trina would fix my coffee for me and she would come over and knock on my trailer and say, 'Harry, coffee's ready...come on over and have some.' Danny did the one-finger stand, which has always impressed me. I know how it's done...but I ain't never going to do no one finger stand.

"Trina didn't like me at first...because I first announced them in the ring as the 'silent film stars.' They were in their sixties...but both of them were classy looking...and had done bits in movies years ago. Anyway, she got upset because of me introducing them as 'silent film stars' but we became very good friends and she always treated me well.

"In Plymouth, New Hampshire, we had a clown join us...his real name was Carmen Scarlotti...he was a great clown. He and I became simpatico right quick. I have always like covered bridges and we used to go look at covered bridges in New Hampshire. Anyway, we're setting-up in this old beat-up ball field in Plymouth, with old run-down bleachers...it was awful...and the top didn't get in, and that meant that the generator truck didn't get in. Of course, without the generator we had no lights. So...DuVal and Trina had this little generator on the back of their trailer rig and DuVal says, 'Well, Harry, we can fool around and rig up some kind of lights together.' We played that spot without a top and with put-together lights...and about three hundred people came out to that open air show. Another time we deliberately did not put up the top, that was in Housatonic, Massachusetts. About ten miles from there was a beautiful little town, Great Barrington, Massachusetts...it had all these Japanese plum trees downtown. I went into a nice little restaurant there and had lunch. When I came out I looked across the park to a theater. It was a theater that I had played with Johnny Cates back in 1959 as Frankenstein.

"I worked with a big time act on this circus named Ken Sherbourne. He came over and joined us for two weeks. Years earlier, he had been on the Ed Sullivan show like eleven times or so. He was about fifty-five and there was nobody as personable and gentlemanly as Ken Sherbourne. He did an act on one of those great big, tall unicycles. I called it a two-story unicycle because it looked that high when he was up there on it juggling flame torches. He also juggled machetes too...and those things were sharp too. He was class, not just in the ring, but in the backyard...when he got up in the morning...he was classy all the time.

"As I said, I was the ringmaster and magician on this show...doing two sets a day. The first half of the show I'd do all the announcing and six minutes of magic, of course we had an intermission, announce the first couple of acts, do magic, and then announce the closing act. A circus is simply a theater under canvas and the ring is the stage.

"We closed in Freehold, New Jersey, six weeks later, just six miles from where we had opened the tour. It's always astounded me how that route worked out, we opened and closed in towns just six miles apart.

"In '84, '85 and '86, I went out with Tommy Lunsford's 'Tommy Tyme Circus.' This was strictly a no-canvas, one truck show...an indoor show...it was then based out of Milledgeville, Georgia. We worked all over Georgia and Tennessee playing school auditoriums, armories, local civic centers, but always worked under a sponsor. They didn't have any elephants...you don't want to take elephants in those indoor places...they'd tear up the floor or damage the door facings or no telling what. It was an easy show to move because we didn't have all that canvas, stakes, center poles, ropes and sidewalls and all.

"I got off the circus in late '86...well I got side-tracked with another woman and that didn't help...but I won't get into that...and I was getting a little tired of the road anyway. I guess the main thing is that ever since I saw that Wallace Brothers circus when I was ten years old, I needed to get it out of my system...it just took me forty years to get around to doing it.

Chapter 10

"The Dreamers Resting Place."
H.W.W. 1983

There is another side to Harry Wise beyond being a magician, ringmaster, wizard, and showman extraordinaire. It is possibly the most mysterious side of his life; the part that goes beyond the theater stage and circus ring. This discovery was made when I came across two, well-worn, limited edition paperback books distributed by Collegiate Distributors of Los Angeles. One is titled "Fragments of Forever" published in 1983, and the other, "Xanadu and You," printed in 1984. Both are collections of prose, sonnets, and poetry from an author named "H. W. Wise." In addition I found four other enchanting works simply signed, "H.W.W." and titled, "Cicadas Serenade", "Goddess Encounter," "Secrets of Ravenslair," and "The Reality of It All." Of course, my immediate question was, could H. W. W. and H. W. Wise be Harry Wise the magician? Or someone else? From the piece titled "Cicada's Serenade" is found the following telltale sign:

"Why, why can't it all be one
Big Beautiful Circus all the time...
Why in the Hell do we always have to suffer all the
Horseshit between dates?"

Now if that doesn't sound like Harry Wise I don't know what does, even though it seems a little curious that he never mentioned anything about writing books. Perhaps a secret had been uncovered that the Wizard did not want disclosed. Intrigue is always fun, and wizards are full of it. There's no doubt that Wise the Wizard is the writer because in

"Fragments of Forever" is found the name "Ray Darkvale." When asked about these works, Wise readily admitted to being the author. It was an unexpected dimension to his life that needed exploration, albeit a bit more mystic than theater magic and ghost shows. Throughout this collection of parables and poems are found esoteric metaphors into which Wise has woven the meanings of life according to his own observations and dreams. Some are clearly cryptic, requiring a little more effort to understand, but the meanings are there for anyone "wise' enough to figure them out.

In November 1971, during his Darkvale period, Wise penned a rather puzzling entry in his diary. Several years later he included it in "Fragments of Forever." Like many of his writings, it is decipherable only by him, or those few who truly know his history, or perhaps by you since the clues are scattered within the pages of this book. Of course we must realize that trying to decipher the secrets of a wizard is not an easy task. The following example is the easiest one to decipher...except everyone who reads it draws a different meaning from it.

Sunday, Nov. 12, 1971, 12:07 a.m.
"The magician Ray Darkvale is dead and buried now. His notes follow as my last legacy to his memory...for I have glimpsed that which he knew!
I will follow soon...I MUST...search for and FIND his dream world of Xanadu!
I know three things...the beautiful girl actually exists...The bridge, river and mill are there at Mansfield, and...I looked across the river and saw the Unicorn too.
After I follow on my best friend's DREAM QUEST, The only one left to know of any of this...If it matters to anyone at all, will be...Alan Milan! The roaring fire is now merely glowing embers. Sleep is overtaking me...I must rest now."

Ray Darkvale was the stage name and alter ego of Harry Wise in the early seventies, but what is this business about Darkvale being dead and buried? Some say it is a mystical suicide letter while others say it is cryptic instructions for an illusion. Maybe you can figure it out but don't expect the Wizard to clue you in. And "Alan Milan"…that was Don Davison's show name, the man who rescued Wise following a devastating romance and inspired him to become "Hans Vogler the mentalist." This can get confusing…two people using so many names.

Wise also mentions "…the bridge, river and mill at Mansfield." If you go back and read Chapter 9, about the time he left the circus in Indiana, you will quickly figure out that he is referring to Mansfield, Indiana. The only problem is, the entry in the Diary was dated 1971, and that is a *fact*, but Wise did not visit this place until 1982, and that is a *fact* too. Either he is clairvoyant, a time-traveler, or just made a great big mistake with the date. He denies all three and will only say that his thoughts come to him late at night, as evidenced by the time of the diary entry. Now recall his remark in Chapter 9, about how his visit to Mansfield was like déjà vu. Does he mean that he dreamed about this place eleven years before he went there? Mansfield and Xanadu are used numerous times in his writings as places of mystical quality. And there are magical unicorns all through his prose. His copious references to the mythical unicorn is perhaps a cryptic symbol of our craving for a tiny sparkle of magic in our monotonous nine-to-five world. Let's face it, wizards pursue unicorns through mystical forests while the rest of the human race seems content with pushing a shopping cart around a crowded supermarket or fussing with their lawn mowers.

After attempting to decipher the hidden meanings in his curious prose and poems, I asked him, "When and how, or what, inspired you to pick up a pen and start writing?" What he told me not only made sense…it took me into another dimension where only wizards can go and come at will…but so can the rest of us if we dare to venture down that narrow, mystical path between reality and fantasy.

"It really started in 1982," explained Wise the Wizard, "when I took that leave from the circus in Indiana, to visit the Lunsford winter quarters in Greencastle. It was my friends Laura and Richard Lunsford, that urged, literally begged me to visit them. They kept telling me about a special…well…a haunted place.

For two solid weeks I refused their invitation. But how could I have known when they told me of this place…how could I have possibly known the enchantment that awaited me? I finally gave in and tagged along with them just to quiet their insistent babbling about a place, that in my mind, was probably no more extraordinary or beautiful, than any other place I had ever been.

"We arrived there in the twilight of an August evening in 1982, and rounding a bend on an old country road, I spied…just ahead…the most fabulous covered bridge ever my eyes beheld. I stood transfixed, awed by its mystery and grandeur. I knew, deep within my spirit, that I had been there before. It was like a dream world. Yet inexplicably, I was also aware that this was my first visit to their glorious bridge. Laura interrupted my sustained stare, 'Come Wise the Wizard and see the old mill up stream. The local folks say it's haunted.'

"We entered the bridge's historic span, crossed the ancient, sturdy planks, and exited the bridge's cover only to be brought up short once again. There, up stream, was the most beautiful old world vision I had ever seen…a stately old mill, three stories tall, gently framed by a thicket of trees where the water roared through the old millwheel. As if struck by enchantment's wand, I was in another world…in another time. It was a rendezvous with destiny…and I felt the enchantment. That's the only way I can express it.

"I returned to that mill for the next three days…I sat on the porch with John Bridgewater, the caretaker of the mill and talked with him. It was built in 1824 and was still in operation and he took me through the mill and gave me the tour. I went over to see him a couple of times and people would come in for a tour of the mill. So I asked him if I could give the tour and guide visitors through the mill. He asked if I knew the story well enough to tell it, I said I got it when you took me through. So, with the permission of Mr. Bridgewater, I was allowed to guide a few visitors through the historic mill. Yes, 'Bridgewater' was really his name and, let me add, very appropriate for this place of mills, rivers and covered bridges. There's thirty-five covered bridges in that county. I found that I could sit on the river between the covered bridges and that mill, and let my imagination work…I'd look at the fields and forests, and across the river…and I could just place unicorns all around…I'm serious…it's a natural unicorn gathering place. That's why I called it the dreamers resting place. In the last days of my stay in that area I knew then that I would finally give in, or give up, to the esoteric fancies of a lifetime...I would write and so I did.

"In *Fragments of Forever* I spoke about my parents taking me to the circus in 1944 where I saw a lariat spinner. Thirty-eight years later I met Richard's father, *Red Lunsford*, then in the prime of his eighty-fourth year. Imagine when I discovered to my surprise and delight, that Red Lunsford was the lariat spinner, whip expert and sharpshooter, that I had seen on the Wallace Brothers circus in my hometown of Sanford, Florida, when I was ten years old! I remembered his grand performance and he had always been a fantasy of mine. Some kind of strange fate had brought us together thirty-eight years later. Think about what a strange twist of fate that was for me, I had literally come full circle from that first circus that I had seen as a kid to another place in time. It was like the past and present connected by all my milestones in between. Coincidence or Fate? Who can say, but certainly a fantasy had become reality. This happens to a lot of people, but they may not be sensitive enough to realize it, or too dumb to see it.

"Now we get to this. That enchanted place that Richard and Laura took me to was Mansfield, Indiana. They were the ones who, unknowingly, introduced me to the circus man of my 1944 childhood dreams. I find all this incredibly ironic, somewhat mystic...somewhat appropriate. Whether it was déjà vu or something else, it was like I had been there before. I had truly found the dreamers resting place. Considering all of this...who could possibly choose reality?

WHERE DREAMS COME TRUE!!

ALL KIDDIE RIDES ½ PRICE

LaVance Amusements

America's Fun Midway

15 Thrilling Rides & Shows!!

FREE PETTING ZOO!!

COME TO THE FAIR   COME TO THE FAIR

The Carousel of the Mystical Unicorn

6 BIG DAYS FEB 5ᵀᴴ thru 10ᵗʰ
Tasbem County Fairgrounds

F. W. LAVANCE SHOWS INC.

80.

Chapter 11

"When you lose your dreams, you die."
Flashdance 1983

Fantasy and reality come in many forms and are often intertwined and difficult to separate, and sometimes downright unexplainable. Reality is often fantasy and sometimes fantasy turns out to be reality. There is a certain amount of magic that is reality, and a certain amount that is fantasy, the trick is never letting the audience know where one stops and the other begins. The same thing is true with legends. Most legends have a real basis, enhanced by fantasy, but the problem is knowing how much is real and how much is fantasy...or perhaps all of it could be real even though it looks like fantasy. An example of this may be in a legend told by Harry Wise.

"There was this blind woman," recounts Wise, "Ramona, was her name, and she remembered going to a carnival as a child...a fair...of course a fair. It all came rushing back to her as she remembered. Her mother had taken her to the fair when she was six. Ramona could not see, but could feel, she could smell, all the sights and sounds around her...the music...the enchanting music stopped her in her tracks. She turned her head, fascinated and drawn to the sounds. 'Take me to the music' she begged her mother. They made their way through the crowd as the music grew louder to her ears. 'Mommy what's making that beautiful music?' It was the merry-go-round. She could sense the bigness of it, the magnificence of it and could feel its pulsing vibration, whirling, spinning, the whole movement of it. Her mother explained about the horses going round and round...as the music played. She begged to ride the carousel and her mother placed her upon one of the horses. At first, before the ride began, she held on

81.

tightly...then deciding to explore, she began caressing her magical steed, and then leaned to touch the horses on her left and right...then hers again. 'Mommy, you've found me a special one!' she exclaimed. 'It has a point, a spike in its head...he's very different from the others. What kind of horse has a spike?'

'A unicorn dear' replied her mother.

'A unicorn!! What color is my unicorn?'

Her mother explained that it was white, all shining white with big dark eyes and a beautiful golden point, like real gold.

The music started and the circling began, up and down, up and down, and around. The thrill of it all made her feel she could fly. She could feel the wind through her hair and she was smiling, laughing...a beautiful, sightless child of six, enchanted for really the first time in her life.

The fair had only two nights left...both of which she had returned to ride the unicorn again and again. Ramona recalled an eerie experience that happened on the last night. She was once again exploring the unicorn with her hands...moving from its ears, over the head, down over the eyes to the mouth. But the hand-carved mouth was different somehow...larger, longer...maybe a little more open? She exclaimed to her mother, 'He's smiling, my unicorn is smiling!!' Her mother's eyes focused on the wooden creature's mouth and in a state of almost disbelief, she agreed...this beautiful carousel unicorn was indeed smiling.

After Ramona told me of her childhood experience at the fair I was reminded of the old Black Horse Legend on the old O. C. Buck Shows. That carnival had a black horse on the merry-go-round that O. C. Buck believed brought good luck. He would always have the ride man to stop the merry-go-round with the black horse facing the window of the office wagon.

I was struck by Ramona's story and decided to write some letters, make a few calls, and look through a stack of old *Amusement Business* magazines just to see if I could find out something about the unicorn. I also checked my copy of *"A History Of The Carousel."* I'm glad that I did, for my discovery was quite incredible. The carousel unicorn remembered by this blind woman, had been on the carousel of the R. R. Royson Shows for forty-one years. At the time of my inquiry, the carved animal was one hundred and two years old. Although R. R. had the carousel for forty-two years, he added the unicorn a year after buying the ride. The wooden animal had been purchased from an old German showman, then in his nineties. R. R. Royson swore from the day it was installed on his carousel that it brought him good luck. The story was very similar to the black horse on the O. C. Buck Show...but this one was a unicorn.

R. R. told me himself that he knew there was something special about his unicorn. He said that in forty-one years it had never been painted. It never had to be...as it always stayed bright and shining as the day he installed it on the ride.

I went to Royson's old winter quarters on a farm outside of Douglas, Georgia, arriving there on an October afternoon. I had called to let the caretaker know that I was coming. When I arrived, about four-thirty in the afternoon, no one was around. However, I was drawn toward an old barn. I opened the squeaking door and literally stepped into another world. There, across from me, to my right, was the abandoned carousel. I stood still for a moment giving my eyes a chance to adjust to the dimness. It was then that an almost mystical thing occurred...a shaft of sunlight beamed through from the loft above, shining on a white unicorn. It was facing straight ahead between two dusty old carousel horses.

I heard a noise behind me and turned to see the old winter quarters caretaker standing there. I told him who I was and he pulled up two canvas chairs and we sat there talking for about an hour. He told me how old Royson had instructed his carousel operator to always stop the ride so the Unicorn would always face his office trailer. Royson wanted to be able to see it from his window. I recalled how O. C. Buck had done the same thing with his black horse!

I hesitantly spoke of the legend I had heard from Ramona, and how she said that the Unicorn had smiled. He told me that he had heard the same thing but that it always happened to a blind, crippled, or deaf child who had been astride it. At this moment...the strangest thing happened...and I can't explain it. There was a squeaking...a grating-like noise from the direction of the old carousel. We turned and saw that, somehow, the Unicorn had made a full half turn toward us. We looked straight into its eyes. There was no explanation for this...whatsoever!!!

Somewhat shaken, I slowly stood up and walked over to it. I reached out and touched it...warmth...that hand-carved animal was warm to my touch. I stood there talking to the Unicorn, telling it I knew and understood. The caretaker stepped closer and pointed to the Unicorn's large black onyx eye. There appeared to be a tear that ran down its long face...and dropped to the carousel deck. We just looked at each other. Twelve years alone in that old barn, it had been twelve years with no special children to ride it.

I later returned to Douglas, Georgia, to the old winter quarters for the purpose of dismantling the mysterious Unicorn. I put it in my trailer and hauled it to Greencastle, Indiana, to be installed on an operating carousel owned by LaVance Amusements, a small nine ride show. After all, this Unicorn was created to be ridden by special children.

Eighteen years later, the LaVance carnival was playing in Herron, Illinois. Whether it was coincidence, fate, or whatever, Ramona was living there after moving from Florida. She knew about the Unicorn being on the LaVance carousel and wanted to relive a childhood fantasy.

Saturday was kids day, the last day of the fair, Ramona entered the midway at 10 a.m. with Druid, her seeing-eye dog. She heard a bus load of children arriving, and from what she could hear, they were from an institution...crippled children. She could hear their exuberance. It brought back memories of when she had gone to the fair as a blind child.

As she stood there listening to the kids and taking in the sounds of the midway, a sudden wind came up blowing sand into her face. Druid began straining at his leash...trying to pull her along the midway. The wind became stronger...it began to worry her...then a far off ominous roar. No, it couldn't be a tornado. She began to panic...tugging at Druid...as he guided her off the main midway...right next to the carousel. It was standing still. Reaching out she touched a carved horse and then felt her way upon the deck of the carousel. She felt each animal until she came to the Unicorn. She could see it through her hands, there was no doubt it was the same beautiful Unicorn from her childhood.

The wind grew stronger as canvas tops flapped and people began running, yelling "tornado!!" Ramona could not move, she stayed right there hugging tightly to the Unicorn. The carousel began trembling and shaking all around her. She could hear those kids and yelled out for them to come to her.

The storm raging now...a cacophony of noise and destruction going on all around her then....a little boy's voice...pleading with Ramona to hold him. She swept him up into her arms and placed him upon the back of the Unicorn and told him to hang on. At that precise moment, with a strong, whipping gust of wind, the carousel began moving in a circular motion...animals going up and down and around as the gears turned, the music began playing. Then all of a sudden, the wind stopped, the roaring ceased, and the carousel came to a slow halt. At no time was there a human agent involved with the turning of the carousel, although people said it was the wind that did it.

All around trucks were overturned, rides and concessions were ripped apart, and the Ferris Wheel was a tangled mass of useless steel. The devastation was almost total, only the carousel and office trailer were untouched by the storm. Strangely, the carousel had stopped with the Unicorn facing the office window...just like in the old O. C. Buck black horse legend. Ramona later recounted her second experience with the enchanted carousel Unicorn...and assured me that once again she felt a smile on his mouth.

High insurance rates and new regulations forced the LaVance carnival to fold in 1990. In 1997, Fred LaVance auctioned off his carved carousel animals. Those old antique carousel animals bring a nice sum today. The Unicorn was purchased by a woman. It now stands in the foyer of her home, still bright and shiny as it was when carved by a master-craftsman over a century ago in Germany. That woman is Ramona, nevermore will she be separated from the Unicorn of her childhood.

Dreams are fantasies that anyone can turn into reality if they have the will to do it. I made all my dreams come true, I've been a house painter, Frankenstein, Mr. Old Stag complete with antlers, Mr. Magic on television, Darkvale, Hans Voglar the mentalist, and a circus ringmaster for three different circuses. I'm reminded of that movie, *Flashdance*, where the man says to the girl, 'When you lose your dreams you die.' I saw that movie four times just to hear that line. I never lost my dream...I stayed with it. I had an eight phase career as a showman...and I'm thankful for that, and of course, many people helped me, my parents and many friends. There was no life like it...when you have twelve or fourteen hundred people around you in the center ring, laughing, and applauding at what you're doing...there's just nothing like it in the world. Life is a stage upon which we all perform, and in the end, we can only hope that we have given our best performance.

Enchanted Glen

For Denise, the most beautiful floating lady any
magician could ever wish to present to an audience.
H. W. Wise

In the early morning mists…

As I stepped to the edge of the forest, there at the clearing, I found myself in a small glen.
I have since come to name it…the Enchanted Glen.

I couldn't believe the VISION there before me…
for standing next to a very small lake was truly the most beautiful girl I ever beheld…she was so tall, slender and graceful…

Regal…yes, regal is the word for her. The vision of her alone was most impressive…but what struck me was all the animals…all the little creatures of the forest were there…with her…or for her.

They were all surrounding her…

All looking up at her…reveling,
yes, actually reveling in the presence of HER.

Each one basking in the radiance of her aura…the rainbow of her eyes and magic of her smile, actually rejoicing in the music of her voice and laughter.

It was all so very unbelievable! Astounding! Impossible! For yes…the *UNICORNS WERE THERE TOO*!!

I MUST,
I WILL,
I am going to return there! I MUST!
I ABSOLUTELY <u>MUST</u> *RETURN!*

From the writings of H. W. Wise.

FRAGMENTS OF FOREVER,
At the Edge of Memories. 1983

Dream Unfair

This dream…this ever recurring dream
                    …that haunts so UNFAIR.
Always drawing me from civilization's
                    …ungodly glare.
Beautiful you
        and the Unicorn are always there.

Sometime soon…
        I will not awaken when the time
                    …comes to finally dare.

I'm going there Now…
                    …to that enchanted place.

Where I once beheld the Unicorn's grace.

This time I shall remain FOREVER…
                    …dreaming not of the unicorns,

but the magic of YOUR celestial face.

                            H.W.W.

From the writings of Harry Wise:

The Squirrel

H. W. Wise

It's the peanut butter that did it, there's no doubt, no doubt whatsoever...I know it for a fact...if it hadn't been for the peanut butter, that very special little squirrel would have never led me to the...well...to that which I'd been seeking.

He seemed already pretty tame, we made friends the first day I arrived to set up camp, when I threw him the first piece of bread, he immediately scampered up the tree with it, he did, however, stay on the lower limb as he ate it...and promptly returned for another piece...by the end of the second day, he was coming right onto the picnic table to ask for his snack. I had Ritz crackers and...peanut butter...over which he immediately went nuts { *no pun intended* }, needless to say by the third day we were buddies.

It was on the fifth and sixth days it happened....

On day five I'd come in late, just before dark...after hiking and yes, searching for my quest...well, there he was scampering down his tree trunk, jumping upon the table and in his usual "squirrel talk squawk" asking for snacks...I stepped into my trailer, and not thinking, left the door open, at which invitation, Mr. Squirrel hops inside right behind me...I saw him and telling him snacks in just a moment, started opening the peanut butter...at the same instant noticing he'd stopped dead still and was staring at the wall...a couple of squawks......and he gingerly leaped upon the cushions next to the table, then a couple of cautious steps across the table he sat back on his haunches and stared absolutely transfixed at the unicorn poster I had there. Suddenly, the little guy became very agitated, and running to my side of the table, started squawking a mile-a-minute...squawking and running in an almost mindlessly senseless circle retracing his agitation from the poster to me over and over again...seemingly oblivious to the aroma of peanut butter filtering through the small reach of my hide-a-way. I lay his favored snack before him...stopping his whirling and circling and catching my eye in a quick glance, he jumped from the table to cushions to floor and out the door...off into the woods faster than lightning!

Baffled, to say the least, I simply ate, turned on the radio news, and began working on *"Dream Friends,"* a collection of short stories sparked from an idea my mom had given me.

The morning of the sixth day came very early...I awoke to all kinds of noise, squawking, running, and scampering over the roof of my trailer...then...all of a sudden, on my screen door, the little squawking devil was running up and down the screen...squawking and gibbering endlessly...the whole time I'm trying to get on my shirt and trousers.

As I opened the door...he darted for the woods, leaving me standing in my usual morning stupor...he comes back, looks at me curiously, rears back...squawks...turns and heads off again and...I'm still standing in my morning...idiot stupor!! Amazed...this time he comes back and grabs my pant leg and starts pulling at it...I finally got the message and start to follow him...Yes, here I was following this little guy deeper and deeper into the woods...*not yet aware of why*...not yet aware that this gentle little forest creature was leading me...actually leading...to what he had seen on my poster!!

He knew...*HE ACTUALLY KNEW*...what he had seen on my trailer wall...*am I assuming too much or did he take off the night before to get permission to bring a mortal to be part of an enchanted encounter there in his forest??* For now I heard the stream where I'd been two days before...we were upstream from a beautiful old covered bridge by about half a mile...and...and...as we broke into the clearing on the stream bank...looking across to the other side...

THERE STOOD THE UNICORN!!!

Other books by Charlie Carlson
📖📖📖
Strange Florida, The Unexplained and Unusual.
Florida's folklore of strange phenomena and oddities.

When Celery Was King.
History of celery farming in Central Florida.

From Fort Mellon to Baghdad.
A time line of the 2nd U.S. Dragoons.

The First Florida Cavalry Regiment, C.S.A.
The history of a Florida Confederate cavalry regiment.

Swedish History of Seminole County, Florida.
Co-authored with Christine Kinlaw-Best and Teri Patterson.

Curious Files of Seminole County, Florida.
Curious stories and folklore from Central Florida.

Bookertown, A journey to the past.
History of an Afro-American town co-authored with Charlie Morgan.

I Got My Dress-tail Wet in Soda Water Creek.
The story of Gladys Hawkins, a Florida Cracker girl growing up in the town of Lake Monroe, Florida.

History of Monroe.
History of a small Central Florida town co-authored with Christine Kinlaw-Best.

Sanford As You Never Knew It.
A souvenir cartoon book celebrating Sanford, Florida's 125th Anniversary.

Memories of Seminole County Families.
Co-authored with Christine Kinlaw-Best and Teri Patterson.